"*Holy Currency Exchange* is steeped in faith, bursting with creativity, and culturally rich. This volume will assist any missional faith enterprise to connect to the blessings that will position them to be used beyond their wildest imagination. Eric H. F. Law is a gifted giver of gifts. He is a gift."

> — Gregory Vaughn Palmer, Resident Bishop,
> West Ohio Conference, the United Methodist Church

"Building on *Holy Currencies*, Eric Law offers a hundred brief reflections on how congregations can leverage their assets as truth-tellers, neighbors, leaders, and hosts to become engines of grace and renewal in their own neighborhood, and rediscover themselves as followers and agents of Christ. I highly recommend this kaleidoscope of essays for anyone interested in embracing the connection to which we are called as communities of faith."

> — Thomas E. Breidenthal, Bishop,
> Episcopal Diocese of Southern Ohio and Author,
> *Christian Households: The Sanctification of Nearness*

"As churches I serve work to make sense of their ministry in today's much changed world, *Holy Currencies* is the book that I have found most helpful to them. *Holy Currencies* is a great tool for assessment and engagement. *Holy Currency Exchange* brings the work of *Holy Currencies* to light and to additional practical reality."

> — Marcia J. Patton, Executive Minister,
> Evergreen Association of American Baptist Churches

"I am a huge fan of the mind and heart of Eric H.F. Law. He has offered the Church a special lens through which to look at the blessed challenge of building multiracial, multiethnic, multicultural communities of faith that genuinely honor the gift of diversity. I have had the pleasure of listening in at conferences and other gatherings in which Eric tested the power of *Holy Currencies*. The practical collection of stories, songs, actions, and visions that are gathered in *Holy Currency Exchange* are a pastor's dream. Here is where the giftedness of an artist, excellent listening skills, and a nimble mind have been combined to share stories, poetry, music, and practical tools and exercises that can transform our ministries. Each clergy should have this on her shelf."

> — Jacqueline Lewis, Senior Minister,
> Middle Collegiate Church, New York

"Elucidating! In *Holy Currencies* we learned the "why" of an alternate way to understand, evaluate, and cultivate a community's gifts for effective deployment. Now in *Holy Currency Exchange,* we are given direct examples of the 'how' to route our way forward and spark the imagination. Thank you, Eric, for another valuable instrument in the leader's tool box."

> — Bruce Barkhauer, Director, Center for Faith and Giving,
> Christian Church (Disciples of Christ)

Other Books by Eric H.F. Law

The Wolf Shall Dwell with the Lamb:
A Spirituality for Leadership in a Multicultural Community

The Bush Was Blazing but Not Consumed

Inclusion: Making Room for Grace

Sacred Acts, Holy Change:
Faithful Diversity and Practical Transformation

The Word at the Crossings:
Living the Good News in a Multicontextual Community

Finding Intimacy in a World of Fear

Holy Currencies: 6 Blessings for Sustainable Missional Ministries

Available at ChalicePress.com

HOLY CURRENCY EXCHANGE

101 Stories, Songs, Actions, and Visions of
Missional and Sustainable Ministries

Eric H. F. Law

CHALICE
PRESS
ST. LOUIS, MISSOURI

Bible quotations, unless otherwise marked, are from the New Revised Standard Version Bible, copyright 1989, Division of Christian Education of the National Council of the Churches of Christ in the United States of America. Used by permission. All rights reserved.

Scripture quotations marked KJV are from the *King James Version*.

Cover design: Scribe, Inc.
Cover art: File licensed by www.depositphotos.com/daksel.

ChalicePress.com

Print: 9780827215016   EPUB: 9780827215023   EPDF: 9780827215030

Library of Congress Cataloging-in-Publication Data

Law, Eric H. F.
Holy currency exchange : 101 stories, songs, actions, and visions of missional and sustainable ministries / by Eric H.F. Law. — First [edition].
    pages cm
Companion to author's Holy currencies.
ISBN 978-0-8272-1501-6 (pbk.)
1. Missionary stories. 2. Missions. I. Law, Eric H. F. Holy currencies. II. Title.

BV2087.L38 2015
253—dc23   2015033128

Printed in the United States of America

Contents

* Includes song. See kscopeinstitute.org for information about obtaining recordings of songs.

---

* Includes song. See kscopeinstitute.org for information about obtaining recordings of songs.

---

* Includes song. See kscopeinstitute.org for information about obtaining recordings of songs.

Acknowledgments

As an author, I am always apprehensive about creating a model of ministry and having to put it down on paper, as I did with the "cycle of blessings" from my last book, *Holy Currencies: Six Blessings for Sustainable and Missional Ministries.* I will wonder: Have I tested the model enough to know that it really works in different contexts? Have I missed anything that is crucial to the comprehensiveness of the model? Luckily, I have had many occasions to continue to work with the material with local churches and ministries since the book was published. Yes, the model continues to work. And, yes, there is more to learn and explore with this resource. The stories, actions, and visions in this book are the results of the exchanges with the good and faithful people who invested their currencies of time and money to attend Holy Currencies workshops.

I give thanks to all the people who embody the cycle of blessings, making the model real and relevant. I especially thank the following people for granting me permission to include their stories and/or their writings in this book: Michael Cunningham, Deborah Dunn, Darla Sloan, Lili Bush, Jeannie Johnson, Heather Leslie Hammer, Donna McCorquodale, Alison Fischer, Jason Fischer, Jeff Sorrell, John Staten, Marcia Patton, Sandy Tice, Amy Smith, Renee Kern, Peter Schell, and Rondesia Jarrett.

I thank my friends and colleagues who refer me to books and resources that connect and support the cycle of blessings—especially Ann Ewen and Mark Edwards for giving me the book *Finding Flow* by Mihaly Csikszentmihalyi. I also want to thank two wonderful bookstores—McNally Jackson in New York City and Vroman Bookstore in Pasadena, California—for consisting displaying books of interest to my research over the years.

I am grateful for the Associates and Catalysts of the Kaleidoscope Institute, who embraced Holy Currencies and invested their time and gracious leadership to learn to share this resources with an ever-widening circle of people in the United States and Canada; they are John Beck, Leroy Chambliss, Bill Cruse, Kristina Gonzalez, Ray Hess, Stacy Kitahata, Lucky Lynch, Patricia Millard, Jake Pomeroy, Randy Stearns, Denise Trevino, Linda Young, Michal Cunningham, Karl Shadley, Bill Shreve, Joanna Shreve, Chuck Greenleaf, Win Fernald, Jennifer Murdock, Dixie Fisher, Karl Shadley, Red Burchfield, Diakonda Gurning, Paula Stecker, Joan Beck, Daphne Dody, Steve Gill, Sonya Luna, Barry Petrucci, Becky Wilson, Bill Chu, Karen Noel, Walter Baire, Jon Jacobs, Jeannie Johnson, Mary Lenn Dixon, Annette Winston,

Rose Ann Vita, and Thérèse Samuel. There are many more who I will not have the space to name.

I am grateful for the individuals and churches that have participated in Holy Currencies workshops and Missional Ministries in the Grace Margin trainings in Ohio, California, Michigan, Wisconsin, Tennessee, and Toronto in the last three years. I give thanks for the leadership and organizational skills of the people who covenanted with the Kaleidoscope Institute and coordinated these trainings: Betsy Anderson, Ron Ewart, and Stephen Fetter for organizing a year-long Holy Currencies workshop for the Toronto area; Harris Tay and Bishop Gregory V. Palmer for the West Ohio United Methodist Conference; Greg Bergquist and Bishop Warner H. Brown for the California-Nevada United Methodist Conference; Anita Hendrix for the River Presbytery, Jeannie Johnson and Bishop Don Johnson for the Episcopal Diocese of West Tennessee; Paul Perez for the United Methodist Conferences in Michigan; Walter Baires for the Lutheran Churches in Milwaukee; Jesús Reyes and Bishop Mary Gray-Reeves for the Episcopal Diocese of El Camino Real; and Karl Shadley for the San Francisco Presbytery. I am still learning about the amazing transformations taking place in these churches and ministries that have taken part in the Holy Currency journey.

I thank the Board of Directors of the Kaleidoscope Institute for taking responsibility for envisioning the future of this amazing ministry. I thank my bishops of the Episcopal Diocese of Los Angeles—J. Jon Bruno, Mary Glasspool, and Diane Jardine Bruce—for their unwavering support over the years. Of course, I am always grateful to the staff of the Kaleidoscope Institute for keeping the Institute running while I focused on writing this book, especially Janis Magnuson, our office manager; Lucky Lynch, director of operations and training; and Clare Zabala Bangao, our treasurer. I give thanks for our former director of communication, Kent Steinbrenner, who supported my writing and music ministries from the beginning.

I am grateful for the faithful readers of *The Sustainist,* my weekly blog. They give me incentive and encouragement to write every week. I thank my nieces, Melissa Ng and Fiona Ng, for their dedication in editing and posting the blog weekly.

My gratitude, as always, goes to the staff at Chalice Press, especially Brad Lyons who convinced me to write another Holy Currency book. I am always grateful for their openness to let me include unconventional materials in my books.

Preface

One way to get attention on the Internet is to string words together that are not commonly used in everyday language. This technique works because people can find you simply by typing these unlikely couplings of words into a search engine, such as Google, Yahoo, or Bing. It has been about two years since the book *Holy Currencies* was published. I had been using the term "Holy Currencies" for about three years before that in my blog, *The Sustainist,* and in workshops I have given across the United States and Canada. When I Google "holy currencies" today, I discover pages and pages of references to this two-word phrase, the majority of these references directly connected to me, the Kaleidoscope Institute, and the book. I was also pleasantly surprised to read sermons, study guides, articles on missional ministries, success stories of missional programs, gracious invitations, diagrams, stewardship addresses, and stewardship packets based on the cycle of blessings model as presented in *Holy Currencies.*

The words "holy" and "currencies" do not usually go together, and that is precisely why I put them together—perhaps initially for shock value, which invites people to pay attention. Combining these two words also challenges our assumptions about what is holy and what is currency. The reason we don't think these two words belong together is that most people don't think currencies (referring to money) can be holy.

The Greek word for "holy" is ἅγιος (hagios), which means set apart for (or by) God. The word implies that the thing, person, or place that is holy is different from the world because it reflects the likeness of the nature of God. Merriam-Webster.com defines "currency" as "something that is in circulation as a medium of exchange." Notice that the word "money" is not part of this definition. Money is just one of many media of exchange. In *Holy Currencies,* I proposed that a missional and sustainable ministry must have the dynamic exchanges of six currencies—Money, Time/Place, Gracious Leadership, Relationship, Truth, and Wellness. These currencies by themselves are not necessarily holy. In fact, they can be exchanged for many destructive actions that individuals and systems can do to people and our environment. For these currencies to be holy, they must resemble the likeness of the nature of God. We must utilize these currencies in ways that follow the pattern of God's will and action.

Here is the big issue: being holy relies on one's concept of the Divine. If I believe in a God who only judges and punishes, then holiness means passing judgment and punishing others. If I believe in a God who forgives, then holiness means forgiving. As a Christian, I believe in the just and compassionate God who shows me the pattern of God's will and action in the person of Jesus. At the heart of holy currencies is the consistent choice to exchange our resources according to God's will, following in Jesus' footsteps.

Where did Jesus spend his time, and what was exchanged for his currency of time and place? What was Jesus' relational network and what were the currency exchanges for these relationships? How did Jesus speak the truth, and what did the currency of truth bring to him and others around him in return? How did Jesus manage Sabbath, and for what did his spiritual wellness prepare him? What was the pattern of exchange when Jesus talked about money?

We all have resources—time, place, leadership, relationship, truth, wellness, and money. What makes these resources holy is a dynamic process of exchanging them to empower the cycle of blessings that sustains communities. This book captures real life stories of these holy currency exchanges, most of which emerged out of Christian communities. Some of these stories are not specifically Christian, but I consider them holy because they follow the divine patterns of holy currency exchange.

This book also offers innovative ideas for holy currency exchanges— some of which have never been tried. These ideas are dreams or visions of what can happen if we dare to follow the divine pattern of holy currency exchange. Some stories and ideas are local, in the sense that they address how to use resources locally. Other stories and ideas are global, addressing broader concerns, such as the wellness and truth of the environment, and of national and international communities. Along the way, I provide songs and poems to open your minds, hearts, and spirits to live into the cycle of blessings.

"Holy" and "currencies" may not go together in our minds initially. It is our choice to make our resources holy by exchanging them for things that are of God's will. *What resources are you setting aside to make holy? What stories can you tell about how you have practiced the cycle of blessings?*

I am sure if you type "holy currencies" into your preferred search engine by the time this book is printed, you will find more stories of holy currency exchanges in addition to those included in this book.

Eric H. F. Law
April 2015

Prelude

Praise God from Whom All Blessings Flow

Praise God from whom all blessings flow
Circling through earth so all may grow
Vanquishing fear so all may give
Widening Grace so all my live

Praise God from Whom All Blessings Flow

1

What's in a Name?

In the Western Christian tradition, January 1 is the feast of the Holy Name, celebrating when Jesus was given his name in the traditional Jewish naming ceremony. January 1 is also my birthday, when I was given the name "Hung-Fat"—a transliteration of my Chinese name written on my birth certificate. Yes, this is where my middle initials, H.F., came from.

The word 鴻 (pronounced hòng) means overflowing. The word 發 (pronounced fā) means expanding, and is a word often used to apply to money, as in the new year well-wishing phrase, "Gong Chi Fā Chai." This phrase literally means "congratulation expanding money." My family was poor when I was born and I suppose my parents gave me this name hoping I would bring prosperity to the family. For similar reasons, many Chinese businesses such as restaurants and hardware stores have the same name.

I used to be embarrassed by my name. However, over the years I have learned to appreciate it, because I have re-visioned what it means for me and my life-work. The word 鴻 is a compound word consisting of the words for river (江) and bird (鳥). The image I have is a scene in which fishermen are pulling in a net so overflowing with fish that hovering birds can share the abundance. As for 發, the image I have is of yeast in bread dough causing it to rise to the right shape before it is baked into bread for our nourishment. I have redefined my name as a symbol of living in abundance. My purpose in life is to expand and share the resources given to me and not hold onto them out of fear.

We have different relationships with our names at different times in our lives. I wonder how Jesus related to his name, which means "God delivers." I wonder how he might have struggled with living up to its meaning as he was growing up. I wonder how his name helped him resolve to live his life and carry out his ministry the way he did.

I invite you to ponder your own name—its meaning, the circumstances around how you were named, how it shaped you, how you struggled with it, and how you might reclaim it, re-vision it, or even change it for the coming year.

When the fullness of time had come, God sent his Son, born of a woman, born under the law, in order to redeem those who were under the law, so that we might receive adoption as children. And because you are children, God has sent the Spirit of his Son into our hearts, crying, "Abba! Father!" So you are no longer a slave but a child, and if a child then also an heir, through God. (Galatians 4:4–7)

Name
A Dialogue

Invite members of your community to gather and learn about each other's names.

1. Invite participants to spend time writing down:
   - My name
   - Meaning of my name or a story associated with my name
   - What have been my relationships with my name over time?
2. Invite participants to share.
3. Invite participants to reflect on what they have heard by completing the following sentences:
   > I noticed...
   > I wonder...

2

Song of Simeon

When the time came for their purification according to the law of Moses, [the parents of Jesus] brought him up to Jerusalem to present him to the Lord (as it is written in the law of the Lord, "Every firstborn male shall be designated as holy to the Lord"),... (Luke 2:22–23)

In the traditional ceremony, Jesus was being designated as holy—set apart for God. But there was something special about this child. A man named Simeon, guided by the Spirit, came into the temple, took the child in his arms, and praised God, saying,

"Lord, now you have set your servant free
    to go in peace as you have promised;
For these eyes of mine have seen the Savior,
    whom you have prepared for all the world to see:
A Light to enlighten the nations,
    and the glory of your people Israel."
(Luke 2:29–32 as translated in The Book of Common Prayer)

There was also a prophet, Anna the daughter of Phanuel, of the tribe of Asher... At that moment she came, and began to praise God and to speak about the child to all who were looking for the redemption of Jerusalem. (Luke 2:36a, 38)

Of course, Jesus' parents were amazed by what was being said about him. The exchange of Jesus' life was going to be the transformation of his people and the peoples of the world. The exchanges were gracious leadership, truth, wellness, and relationship based on unconditional love for all.

When we dedicate our lives to be holy, we should not expect anything less than that which Jesus exchanged for his holy living, dying, and rising. We may not know all the ramifications at first, but if we stay on the course of this holy exchange, we will see, as Simeon and Anna saw, that a child dedicated to be holy will be a catalyst for local and global transformation.

The child grew and became strong, filled with wisdom; and the favor of God was upon him. (Luke 2:40)

Song of Simeon

Principal Theme

Mmm._____ God, you now have set your ser-vant free (Lord),

Mmm._____ to go in peace as you have pro - mised.

Tema principal, en español

A - ho-ra des-pi-des Se - ñor a tu sier-vo. Mmm._____ Con-

-for-me a tu pa - la-bra en paz. Mmm._____

Verses: *To be sung by soloists or in a small group.*

For these eyes of mine have seen the Sav - ior, whom

you have pre-pared for the world to see; a light to en-light-en the

na-tions, and the glo - ry of your peo-ple Is - ra - el.

Doxology or Gloria Patri

May be sung to end the piece. Choose either text.

Praise to the ho - ly and un - di - vi - ded__ Tri - ni - ty, One God:__ as
Glo - ry to the Fa - ther and to the Son, and to the Ho - ly Spi - rit: as

it was in the be - gin - ning, is now, and will be for ev - er. A - men.

For Compline, begin with this theme

Guide us wak - ing, O God, and guard us sleep - ing, that a -
(Lord),

wake we may watch with Christ, and a - sleep we may rest in peace.

Add this theme in Easter Season

Al - le - lu - ia. Al - le - lu - ia.

Al - le - lu - ia. Al - le - lu - ia.

Accompaniment 1

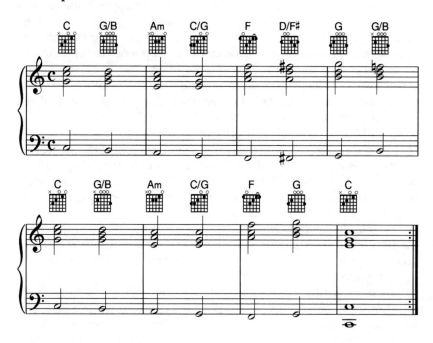

Accompaniment 2

Performance Note: Using these melodies, a music minister can arrange the piece in many different combinations. As an example, if this piece is used in the context of Morning or Evening Prayer, the group can begin the piece by singing the English principal theme. The group can then add the Spanish principal theme. This will become the background chant throughout the whole piece. A soloist can then sing the verses a few times, and a group can add the Doxology or Gloria Patri to end the piece. If this piece is done in the context of Compline—the traditional final prayer service of the day—the group can begin with "Guide us waking . . ." If it is the Easter season, add the "Alleluia." After the English and Spanish principal themes are introduced, the previous two themes should gradually fade out. Then a soloist can add the verses and the Doxology or Gloria Patri. The "Alleluia" may reenter here. Then "Guide us waking . . ." is reintroduced again, while the rest of the themes fade away, leaving the group quietly singing "Guide us waking . . ." to end the piece.

Accompaniment Notes: Only the harmonic structure and the chord progression of the basic unit of each piece is given here. In order to accompany the singing, one only needs to repeat the basic unit continuously, maintaining a steady tempo.

If a guitar is used, it should always be unobtrusive, using plucked chords or arpeggios to provide a steady background of sound, avoiding staccato strums or syncopated rhythms except when called for in the piece.

In a church, the organ or another keyboard instrument will be most useful. Experienced keyboard players are encouraged to improvise on the basic unit, adding to the texture of the piece.

Instruments can be employed either playing the various parts with the congregation, or solo if the instrumentalist can improvise.

3

The Gift

At the beginning of the new year, I often hear people say with a sigh of relief, "Thank God the holidays are over!" I recall seeing frantic shoppers before Christmas trying to find the right presents for people to whom they are obligated to give gifts. If gift giving is reduced to an obligation and is measured as a commodity, I can understand how it would be a relief to be done with it until the next birthday or anniversary or Christmas.

In his now-classic book, *The Gift: Creativity and the Artist in the Modern World,* author Lewis Hyde shares stories from different cultures around the concept of exchanging gifts. He writes:

> These stories present gift exchange as a companion to transformation, a sort of guardian or marker or catalyst. It is also the case that a gift may be the actual agent of change, the bearer of new life. In the simplest examples, gifts carry an identity with them, and to accept the gift amounts to incorporating the new identity.[1]

According to Hyde, there are at least three obligations to gift economy— the obligation to give, the obligation to accept, and the obligation to reciprocate. In many of the cultural stories that Hyde examined, the reciprocation may not go directly back to the original giver but to a third party. Sometimes the gift is expected to keep flowing throughout the community and it may eventually return to the original giver in different forms. Hyde wrote, "[A] gift that cannot be given away ceases to be a gift. The spirit of a gift is kept alive by its constant donation."[2]

For Christians, one of the greatest gifts that we receive is Jesus. To accept this gift is to incorporate a new identity embodied by the words and actions of Jesus. At the baptism of Jesus:

> [J]ust as he was coming up out of the water, he saw the heavens torn apart and the Spirit descending like a dove on him. And a voice came from heaven, "You are my Son, the Beloved; with you I am well pleased." (Mark 1:11)

Jesus taught us, in the Lord's Prayer, to call God "Father." The actual word that Jesus used was "Abba," which was what a child would call his or her parent in the language that Jesus spoke. Jesus, as the catalyst, transforms

---

[1]See Lewis Hyde, *The Gift: Creativity and the Artist in the Modern World* (New York: Vintage Books, 2007), 57.
[2]Ibid., xix.

our relationship with God to that of parent-child relationship. This is the gift, the new identity. We are to reciprocate by giving this gift to others, treating them also as children of God so that the gift can be kept alive and continue to increase and flow through our communities and spread throughout the world.

I invite you to begin each morning with this mantra: "I am a beloved child of God, with whom God is well pleased." Then, as you go through the day, affirm each person you encounter (in your family, neighborhood, workplace, school, etc.) as a beloved child of God by silently saying, "You are a beloved child of God with whom God is well pleased." In some cases, it might be appropriate to say this out loud. When we give this gift to ourselves and to everyone we encounter, we become catalysts who might actually transform the world!

Gift and Identity
A Dialogue

Invite members of your community to gather and learn about each other's experiences of giving and receiving gifts:

- Invite each participant to recall a time when he/she received a gift that helped define his/her identity.
  - Describe the occasion. What was the gift?
  - Who was the giver?
  - How did this gift help you understand or define who you are?
  - What else did you gain beyond the actual gift itself in the process?
  - If you have had the occasion to give the same gift to another later in life, describe that experience as well.

- Invite participants to share their recollections.
- Invite participants to reflect on what they have heard by completing the following sentences:

  - I noticed...
  - I wonder...

4

Love First

During many of my sermons and workshops, I have often asked participants to stand up and approach at least three people and say, "You are a beloved child of God with whom God is well pleased." This activity always seems to connect people very quickly and in meaningful ways. At one particular gathering, a man started crying and said, "No one has ever said that to me before!"

Some of us might think that love is something that we must earn—that is, we have to do something good and pleasing in order to receive love. Some of us might think that we don't deserve such a love because we have done something wrong in the past. Some of us might think that a person who loves us unconditionally doesn't really exist. Some of us might think that it is foolish for a person to love without any conditions, because he or she would be opening him/herself up for abuse.

Yet, Jesus talked about God as someone who loves us first unconditionally. We don't have to earn this love. When we have made mistakes, instead of judging us, God still loves us. We change our ways, but not in order to re-earn God's love. We change because we are loved. This love is given freely without expectation of anything in return. Whether I accept it or not, this unconditional love from God is still there—always there. To receive and accept this love is to embrace love as my core identity. I receive the gift of unconditional love, and in my gratefulness, I can't help but share it, so others can also see it and experience it and acknowledge it.

Therefore, unconditional love is not a currency of exchange. If I trade love as a commodity and expect a return, my offer ceases to be love. Love allows me to know who I am. Love gives me the courage to give of my self and my resources. Love, therefore, is the power source, the spiritual battery that empowers the cycle of blessings. Unconditional love is the foundation of a sustainable community. Offering this love to each other energizes the flow of material, human, spiritual, and natural resources, rejuvenating relationships and creating a gracious, sustainable community.

Beloved, since God loved us so much, we also ought to love one another. No one has ever seen God; if we love one another, God lives in us, and his love is perfected in us. (1 John 4:11–12)

11

5

Love Is My Name

To say that I am made in the image of God is to say that love is the reason for my existence: for God is love. Love is my true identity. Selflessness is my true self. Love is my true character. Love is my name. If therefore, I do anything or think anything or say anything or know anything or desire anything that is not purely for the love of God, it cannot give me peace, or rest, or fulfillment, or joy.[3] — *Thomas Merton*

---

[3]See Thomas Merton, *Seeds of Contemplation* (Norfolk, Conn.: New Directions Books, 1949), 46.

Love Is My Name

6

I Am...

Bill Strickland grew up in the 1960s in Manchester, Pennsylvania—a poor, low-lying inner-city neighborhood in Pittsburgh. In the wake of the assassination of Dr. Martin Luther King Jr. in 1968, Manchester was under siege with racial strife. Strickland, who was just 19 at the time, wanted to provide "a safe, sane, quiet environment where [young people] could escape the madness that reigned in the streets, work on some clay, find a way to shape something personal and beautiful, and spend some time in a bright, clean, nurturing place where it did not seem pointless to dream."[4]

With the help of the Episcopal Church, he founded the Manchester Craftsmen's Guild, a tiny neighborhood art center, to teach young people to make pottery. Thirty years later he is the president and CEO of Manchester Bidwell Corporation, the premier job training and community arts-education center in Pittsburgh. The facility comprises three separate buildings, with 150 people on staff, 1,200 students, and 2,500 young people served by programs in public schools.[5]

During the creation of the Craftsmen's Guild, Strickland discovered what would become the foundation of his later work. He wrote, "...I knew that identity isn't something you inherit, it's something you must discover. The Craftsmen's Guild was helping me discover mine. Who was I? I was the guy who believed that art and creative experience are stronger than fear and ignorance. I was the guy who created this place out of passion and vision and sweat. I built the Guild out of ideas and things that I treasured, or needed, or believed in, and in doing so, I created the kind of personal foundation... crafted from genuine values and passions that would serve as a base for a rich and meaningful life."[6]

Our core identity is what drives us to do amazing and courageous things in our ministries, as demonstrated in the following story from Exodus:

> The king of Egypt said to the Hebrew midwives, one of whom was named Shiphrah and the other Puah, "When you act as midwives to the Hebrew women,...if it is a boy, kill him; but if it is a girl, she shall live. But the midwives feared God; they did not do as the king

---

[4]Bill Strickland with Vince Rause, *Make the Impossible Possible* (New York: Broadway Books, 2007), 7.

[5]Watch a video about Bill Strickland called "The Hope Business" at http://www.youtube.com/watch?v=--_cAUzAHZw&feature=channel_video_title.

[6]Strickland with Rause, *Make the Impossible Possible*, 69–70.

of Egypt commanded them, but they let the boys live. So the king of Egypt summoned the midwives and said to them, "Why have you done this, and allowed the boys to live?" The midwives said to Pharaoh, "Because the Hebrew women are not like the Egyptian women; for they are vigorous and give birth before the midwife comes to them." So God dealt well with the midwives; and the people multiplied and became very strong. (Exodus 1:15–20)

Shiphrah and Puah helped prevent the genocide of male Hebrew infants because they knew who they were and they feared God. They were midwives; their role was to bring lives into the world, not destroy them. Their understanding of identity gave them the courage to disobey the powerful Pharaoh. Because of their conviction, the people continued to grow strong in spite of ongoing oppression.

Just as being a midwife was the rock of courage that enabled Shiphrah and Puah to stand up to the destructive life-depleting power, Bill Strickland built his dream on his foundational identity and over the years helped turn many lives around, providing spiritual, social, and financial sustainability for many individuals and families.

As part of our Holy Currencies training curriculum, we invite participants to complete the following sentences without using church jargon:

- Being a Christian is...
- Being a Christian is not...
- Belonging to the Church is...
- Belonging to the Church is not...

Most church members are quick to respond to what "Being a Christian is NOT" and "Belonging to the Church is NOT," but are slow and even struggle to find words to describe what "Being a Christian IS" and "Belonging to the Church IS." This inability to articulate clearly and readily their identity as individuals and as a community might explain why many church organizations have difficulty reaching and serving people outside their own comfortable circle. Without this foundational identity, many churches also lack the courage to confront injustice. Without this identity, many churches become unsustainable both socially and financially.

Discovering our identity in the context of the diverse and rapidly changing world is the foundation, the rock, on which a sustainable community can be built. When we know who we are, we can have the courage to confront the system that seeks to stop the flow of resources to the powerless and the oppressed. Standing firmly on the rock of our identity in Christ and as the Church, we can work with others to do more with less, recirculate resources, and build a sustainable future together.

Identity
A Dialogue

Gather members of your community for a time of dialogue on "identity."

1. Invite participants to recall an event in their lives that gave them a sense of identity and purpose, particularly in doing good for others, the community, and the world. This could be a moment of recognition facilitated by a mentor, friend, teacher, or family member.
2. Invite each participant to share his/her story. After each story, invite the speaker to complete the sentence beginning with "I am..."
3. Invite participants to further reflect on this dialogue by sharing sentences beginning with:

> I noticed...
> I wonder...

4. Close the dialogue inviting participants to complete the sentence:

> We are...

7

Stewardship of Stories

A few years ago, I was invited to be the speaker at a conference titled "Stewardship of Our Stories." As I planned my keynote address, I realized that in order for a story to be worth anything, it must flow like a currency of exchange. In fact, stories can be part of the currencies of relationship, truth, and wellness. If I have a wonderful story but I don't know I have it and I don't know how to tell it, it is of no use to anyone. So the first step to becoming good stewards of our stories is to know our own stories, especially the ones that sustain life and relationship, and speak the truth. The second step is to learn how to tell the stories authentically. That is, speak from what you hear, see, and feel. Be honest with yourself and share from your heart.

Third, even if I can tell my story, if no one is listening, the story is useless. So, in order to be good stewards of our stories, we need to find or develop an audience.

Fourth, I need to connect my story with the greater story with which others can connect. How is my story part of God's story of love, grace, and truth? How does my story connect with the saints of the past?

Fifth, I can't just walk up to anyone and tell my story, because it may be received and interpreted in any number of ways—some of which might be negative and unproductive. To maximize the currency of stories, I need to create a gracious time and place in which these stories can be received without being prejudged, so that they will bring blessings.

Finally, I need to remind my listeners about the ethical responsibilities that go along with listening to stories. The responsibility might be to pass the story—the gift—along. The responsibility might be to hold the story in confident in support of the wellbeing of the storyteller. The responsibility might be to address the truth that is shared through the story by moving from listening and receiving to action.

Daniel Taylor, in an article in the *Mars Hill Review,* wrote, "Stories tell us who we are, with the understanding that who we are is greatly shaped by the community of which we are a part. (The universal in us is a product of our common humanity as colored by our particular community.) And who we are unavoidably raises the host of ethical questions about how we should live."[7]

---

[7]See the article I found at http://www.leaderu.com/marshill/mhr03/story1.html by Daniel Taylor, "The Ethical Implications Of Storytelling: Giving Ear to the Literature of the Oppressed," in *Mars Hill Review,* issue 3 (Fall 1995): 58–70.

Dr. Martin Luther King Jr., in his *Letter from a Birmingham Jail,* defended and even embraced being labeled as an extremist. Placing his story within the context of the greater story, King challenged his audience (at that time, white religious leaders) to act for love and justice:

> But as I continued to think about the matter, I gradually gained a bit of satisfaction from being considered an extremist. Was not Jesus an extremist in love?—"Love your enemies, bless them that curse you, pray for them that despitefully use you." Was not Amos an extremist for justice?—"Let justice roll down like waters and righteousness like a mighty stream." Was not Paul an extremist for the gospel of Jesus Christ?—"I bear in my body the marks of the Lord Jesus." Was not Martin Luther an extremist?—"Here I stand; I can do no other so help me God." Was not John Bunyan an extremist?—"I will stay in jail to the end of my days before I make a mockery of my conscience." Was not Abraham Lincoln an extremist?—"This nation cannot survive half slave and half free." Was not Thomas Jefferson an extremist?—"We hold these truths to be self-evident, that all men are created equal." So the question is not whether we will be extremist, but what kind of extremists we will be. Will we be extremists for hate, or will we be extremists for love? Will we be extremists for the preservation of injustice, or will we be extremists for the cause of justice?[8]

His passion for the wellness of the people in this nation compelled him to speak the truth of his own experience and the experiences of the African Americans. He created an audience through his relationships with the religious leaders of his time. He knew he had an audience who would listen. And I think he knew that his letter would be shared widely beyond the initial group to which he was addressing it. King's identity and actions transformed a nation, leading its people to reclaim basic human rights and act as if all people really are equal and resources should flow not just within one group, based on skin color, but to sustain all.

Find a time, a place, and an audience today and listen to stories. More importantly, take responsibility for hearing these stories. Then tell your story, and talk about your identity, your passion and how your story (and Dr. King's story) and Jesus' story intersect, empowering your own transformation, moving yourself and others toward actions that create sustainable communities.

---

[8]I found the complete text of the *Letter from a Birmingham Jail* by Martin Luther King Jr. at http://www.uscrossier.org/pullias/wp-content/uploads/2012/06/king.pdf.

8

Year-Round Stewardship

Many church leaders get nervous about finances in the middle of the year. They wonder, "Are we going to meet our budget? If the church's income is not on target, how can we get people to give more during the second half of the year?"

Then, as they approach the last quarter of the year, many churches start their stewardship campaigns, which often focus exclusively on the currency of money. Having "tunnel-vision" when it comes to money leads to ignoring other currencies that may help church leaders make wise decisions for long-term sustainability. This is how churches fall into the scarcity trap: the more the church obsesses over money, the more they narrow the focus and ignore other opportunities and options. They make decisions without the full benefit of the currencies of truth, wellness, and gracious leadership. These decisions, in turn, may cause the church's financial picture to worsen. In this way, the cycle of scarcity continues.

One way to move people out of tunnel mode is to interrupt with reminders of what is important. A group of economists tried to help poor people in Bolivia, Peru, and the Philippines increase their saving. The economists' research showed that the poor fail to save, in part, because of tunneling. "Saving is an important but not urgent task, the kind that nearly always falls outside the tunnel. At any point in time, there are more pressing things to do than save."[9] To bring saving into the scope of vision of the poor, the economists sent them a quick note at the end of each month, reminding them of what they were saving for and how much. These benign reminders boosted savings by 6 percent. "We were able to increase savings not through education or by steeling people's willpower but merely reminding them of something important that they tend to overlook when they tunnel."[10]

One of the biblical images of our role within God's creation is that of a steward who is put in charge of the household while the owner is away (Mark 13:33–37). Because we don't know when the owner will return, we are challenged, as stewards, to stay alert. At any moment, we might need to account for that which has been put in our charge. This alertness should not be limited to a particular time of the year. Therefore, churches should not wait until the last quarter of the year to conduct a stewardship campaign. They should avoid focusing only on the currency of money, which can reinforce

---

[9]Sendhil Mullainathan and Eldar Shafir, *Scarcity* (New York: Picador, 2013), 206–207.
[10]Ibid.

the tunnel effect. Try reminding your community to be good stewards of all of God's currencies—time and place, gracious leadership, relationship, truth, wellness, *as well as* money—through the entire year.

In this book, there are sample pledge cards for all the holy currencies. Use them to interrupt whatever tunneling your church members might be preoccupied with and remind them of what is important in addition to money—the flowing of truth, the exercising of gracious leadership, the networking of relationships, the fostering of wellness, the sharing of our places, and the investment of our time. Use these pledge cards, perhaps once a month, to remind everyone that they can choose to direct these currencies toward the holy, and toward creating a sustainable community through all the days of their lives.

> Think of us in this way, as servants of Christ and stewards of God's mysteries. Moreover, it is required of stewards that they be found trustworthy. (1 Corinthians 4:1–2)

9

Pledge Card for Currency of Relationship

Since the publication of *Holy Currencies,* readers have discovered exciting ways of applying the cycle of blessings, and have challenged me to do the same. One of the recurring requests has been, "We are nearing the traditional time for pledge campaigns and I was wondering if anyone has created 'pledge cards' based on Eric Law's model?" In response, I began to construct the pledge cards based on the cycle of blessings. The goal was to use a familiar medium, the pledge card, to assist members of the church community to value and give other currencies beyond money.

Here is the first of these pledge cards, on the currency of relationship. Built into this card are the internal and external elements that are essential for fully applying each of the holy currencies to ministry. The "accountable person" (mentioned on the card) is someone who will remind me of my commitment. This is also the person to whom I will report when I have fulfilled my pledge.

Look for the other pledge cards for currencies of truth, wellness, gracious leadership, money, and time and place in this book and consider using them as part of your stewardship program. These pledge cards, when used regularly, become tools for teaching the cycle of blessings, transforming the way people think about church from maintenance to missional. Obviously it would be too much to ask church members to commit to all six currencies at one time. The cards are more appropriate for a year-round stewardship approach—perhaps, every two months, invite church members to pledge to one of the currencies.

Make a pledge today to increase your currency of internal and external relationship. Look around your church: Who would you like to get to know better this year? Using the pledge card below, fill in the number of relationships that you would strengthen within your church. Then take a look outside your church—your workplace, your neighborhood, your friendship circle. With whom among them would you like to build a stronger relationship? Remember that we are not talking about evangelism in which you witness to these people. We are inviting you to simply be a friend to listen to their stories and for them to know your story. Find someone who will be your accountable person. When you have fulfilled your commitment, get together with your accountable person and share what exchanges these relationships have given you. Discuss what God is calling you to do with the blessings you received from these relationships.

Pledge Card for Currency of Relationship

- I commit to strengthen ____ relationships I have within my church.
- I commit to establish ____ new relationships outside my church.

My name: _____ My accountable person: _____

_____   _____
      signature   signature

Date: _____

10

I Notice... I Wonder...

In his book *Finding Flow,* Mihaly Csikszentmihalyi says that attention is the most precious resource that we have.[11] Paying attention can make the difference between being stuck in a boring job or finding fulfillment in the same job. "A supermarket clerk who pays genuine attention to customers, a physician concerned about the total well-being of patients rather than specific symptoms only, a news reporter who considers truth at least as important as the sensational interest when writing a story, can transform a routine job with ephemeral consequences into one that makes a difference."[12]

When we pay attention to what we are doing, the people with whom we are doing it, and the environment in which we are doing it, we add value to what we do. When we pay attention, we might discover the truth about the people and environment as they are, and not as we want them to be. We might also be surprised by new ideas, options, and solutions we have not considered. We may discover the reason why we do what we do, and the contributions it makes toward creating sustainable community.

One of the gracious leadership skills we teach at the Kaleidoscope Institute is the completion of the sentences:

> I notice...
> I wonder...

These sentences invite us to pay attention first, and then be curious. Try taking a moment during the day to stop whatever you are doing and complete these sentences. What do you notice about yourself? What do you notice about the environment? What do you notice about the people around you? What do you wonder about yourself, others, and the environment?

Here is another set of questions that can help you learn to pay attention to an event that has happened:

1. What happened?
2. What caused it to happen?
3. What did I learn—about self, others, and environment?
4. What would I do differently next time?

"What happened?" invites you to recall what you noticed. When done in a group, as we ask this question we begin to see the truth from multiple perspectives.

---

[11]Mihaly Csikszentmihalyi, *Finding Flow* (New York: Basics Book, 1997), 103
[12]Ibid.

"What caused it to happened?" invites you to recall the flow of actions that led to the event in question. What were the exchanges? Were the exchanges constructive or destructive?

"What did I learn?" invites you to name the learning—the gift—that you gain from exploring the truth about self, others, and the environment.

"What would I do differently next time?" invites you to choose the path toward the holy next time you find yourself in a similar situation.

I have used this set of questions many times in consulting with organizations and communities that had to learn to tell the truth in order to achieve wellness.

Try this yourself or with a group of people who have just experienced something exciting, challenging, puzzling, or affirming. Take time to work through each question. This set of questions teaches people to pay attention, learn, and discern together.

11

Restoring Trust

I was on a plane from Los Angeles to Philadelphia. The flight was full. On the drive to the airport, I had heard a report on the radio about an Associated Press/GfK poll that found most Americans were suspicious of each other in everyday encounters. Nearly two-thirds of the people polled said, "You can't be too careful" in dealing with people.

On that flight, I happened to be sitting in the exit row. The flight attendant came over to ask if we were willing and able to help in case of an emergency. Of course, I said yes. But then I looked around the enclosed space and it occurred to me that if the poll was correct, two out of three people on the plane didn't trust me. I realized how serious this was: How can a society be sustainable if people don't trust each other? When we don't trust, we don't share our resources, out of fear. When resources don't flow, the community will starve. Perhaps Congress's inability to get things done as well as the "stand your ground" laws that made news after the death of Trayvon Martin are both symptoms of this inability to trust.

A survey of trust in the workplace done by Paul Bernthal, Ph.D., of Development Dimensions International showed that the top five trust-reducing behaviors of a coworker were:[13]

1. Acts more concerned about his or her own welfare than anything else;
2. Sends mixed messages so that I never know where he or she stands;
3. Avoids taking responsibility for actions ("passes the buck" or "drops the ball");
4. Jumps to conclusions without checking the facts first;
5. Makes excuses or blames others when things don't work out ("finger-pointing").

The top five ranked trust-building behaviors were:

1. Communicates with me openly and honestly, without distorting any information;
2. Shows confidence in my abilities by treating me as a skilled, competent associate;
3. Keeps promises and commitments;

---

[13]http://www.ddiworld.com/DDIWorld/media/trend-research/surveyoftrust intheworkplace_es_ddi.pdf?ext=.pdf.

4. Listens to and values what I say, even though he or she might not agree;
5. Cooperates with me and looks for ways in which we can help each other;

Read the two lists again and reflect on how you have behaved during the past week with family members, neighbors, friends, and coworkers. Have you been part of the trust-reducing culture? Have you fostered trust with people whom you encounter each day? How can you enable people around you to embrace practices and processes to build and restore trust, which are essential for developing sustainable communities?

12

Winter Epiphany

Having lived in California for more than 30 years, I have lost much of my sense of the rhythm of the seasons. Trapped in my warm hotel room in Chicago, looking out at the forbidding -45 F (with wind-chill factor) outside, I regained some of the introspection I used to have when I lived on the East Coast. Sometimes, I thought to myself, things need to die in the winter before something new can be born in the spring.

I founded the Kaleidoscope Institute in 2006, growing it from one part-time employee—me—to an organization with many associates who create local learning communities and offer training and resources to local churches and organizations within the major denominations in the United States, Canada, Australia, and Asia. As the founder of this ministry, I have discovered the most profound challenge to be: "How do I let go, so that this ministry may have a life of its own (without me!) and serve more people everywhere?" I became aware of this challenge after I found myself overworked, while the institute had reached a plateau in its ability to meet the needs of our clients and the obligations to our staff.

In the middle of 2013, the board of directors and I went back to the drawing board and restructured our staff. We redesigned our curriculum so it could be facilitated with the same high quality, but would require less training time for teachers. As I looked toward the spring of 2014, I prayed that the new structure and curriculum would enable the institute to become independent of me so that more churches and organizations would benefit from our resources without them having to be delivered by me. My shifting role continues to be difficult, but also rewarding because I know there will be spring. I am glad my colleagues and I are working toward this new vision together.

The world is changing. The organization I created is changing. The people who have the passion for this ministry are changing. So who I am must also be changing. Does that mean I will lose myself? No. It actually requires that I know and am secure about who I am. With this self-knowledge as my foundation, I am free to explore and change, knowing I will not lose my core identity as a beloved child of God.

Do you know who you are as a human being? Do you know who you are in the context of your family and community? Do you know who you are as member of a faith community? Do you know who you are as a citizen of the country to which you belong? Do you know who you are as a child of God? Knowing the truth of your core identity will empower you to explore change gracefully and faithfully.

13

Transfiguration

In the gospel of Mark, God's voice is heard twice. The first time is during the baptism of Jesus, when God says, "You are my Son, the Beloved; with you I am well pleased" (Mark 1:11). The second time is during an event called the Transfiguration, in which Jesus leads his disciples up a high mountain and there they see that "he was transfigured before them, and his clothes became dazzling white, such as no one on earth could bleach them. And there appeared to them Elijah with Moses, who were talking with Jesus" (Mark 9:2b–4). After Peter tries to capture and fix the moment by proposing to build three dwellings for them, the voice of God says, "This is my Son, the Beloved; listen to him!" (9:7b).

The beginning of the year is when Christians celebrate the baptism of Jesus. In chapter 3 of this book, I invited my readers to affirm each person they encountered (in their family, neighborhood, workplace, school, etc.) as a beloved child of God by silently saying, "You are a beloved child of God with whom God is well pleased." Affirming the individual we meet as a beloved child of God is the beginning of a sacred relationship.

To deepen the relationship, we need the second affirmation: this beloved child of God deserves to be listened to. Only by truly listening do we stop ourselves from "fixing" the person in a particular time and place, ignoring the fact that everyone changes with time. Our first impulse may be like Peter's in the Transfiguration story—wanting to hold onto that moment because it seems "good." But listening helps us discern the truth of others as they reveal themselves to us, and as they change.

During this week, as you encounter different people in your daily life, say silently to each person, "You are a beloved child of God and I will listen to you." In some cases, it might be appropriate to say it out loud!

The Spirit of God Has Been Given to Me

"The Spirit of God has been given to me,
For God has anointed me
and sent me to bring good news to the poor:
To proclaim liberty to the captives;
To the blind, new sight;
To set the downtrodden free,
To proclaim the year of God's favor."
(Luke 4:18–19, paraphrased.)

The Spirit of God Has Been Given to Me

Canon

The Spir-it of God has been giv-en to me, for God has a -
noint - ed me and sent me to bring good news to— the
poor:_____ To pro - claim lib-er-ty_____ to the
cap - - tives,_____ to the blind, new sight;
to set the down-trod-den free._____

Descant

The Spir - it of God____

has been giv - en, giv - en to me____

to pro - claim the year of God's fav - or.____

Accompaniment

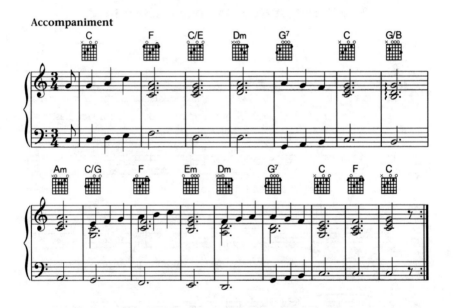

15

Relational Conversation

One of the essential exercises in the Holy Currencies workshop is called "From Task to Relationship."[14] The assignment is to take a ministry that has been task-driven and reimagine it, putting more emphasis on building relationships. This exercise is often the turning point for many church teams who come to the workshop. The shift from being task-oriented to being relationship-oriented often serves as the first step for participants to get a real sense of what it means to be missional. In other words, this initial shift invites church leaders to rethink how they invest their currencies of time, place, and money. Do they exchange these currencies for doing something for others or do they exchange them for building up their currencies of relationship?

At the end of this exercise, after each team reports their relational-missional ministry ideas, participants often ask, "How do you train people to build relationship? We are so used to "doing church" that we don't know how to start a conversation with a stranger." Here is some helpful advice from *Finding Flow* by Mihaly Csikszentmihalyi:

> The secret of starting a good conversation is really quite simple. The first step is to find out what the other person's goals are: What is he interested in at this moment? What is she involved in? What has he or she accomplished, or is trying to accomplish? If any of this sounds worth pursuing, the next step is to utilize one's own experience or expertise on the topics raised by the other person— without trying to take over the conversation, but developing it jointly. A good conversation is like a jam session in jazz, where one starts with conventional elements and then introduces spontaneous variations that create an exciting new composition.[15]

This is how you train church members to have relational conversations. Invite them to pay attention to the other. Find out the other's goals, passions, interests, accomplishments, and concerns. Feed back to the other what you have heard. Tap into your own experiences. Then start a jam session.

---

[14]See Eric H. F. Law, *Holy Currencies* (St. Louis: Chalice Press, 2013), 25–26.
[15]Mihaly Csikszentmihalyi, *Finding Flow* (New York: Basics Book, 1997), 114–15.

16

Training the Inclusive Brain

I have been teaching communities to use the process of "Mutual Invitation" for more than 30 years. Used within a group of five to 12 people, Mutual Invitation ensures that everyone is invited to share, with the option to pass or to pass for now. Much has been said about the effectiveness of the process—it helps people to listen, it honors each person, it builds self-esteem, it puts the powerful and the powerless on the same level. There are now communities that have been practicing this process for an extended period of time, and we are noticing the long-term impact of this process.

One recurring comment goes like this: "Since I have been using Mutual Invitation, I am more aware of who is excluded everywhere I go." In reflecting on this comment, I notice that I, too, am acutely aware of who is included or not in different environments. Perhaps, I am benefiting from the accumulative effect of Mutual Invitation.

Once, I attended a meeting in which only a few people spoke, and the majority did not get a word in. At the end of the meeting, I asked the leader, "How did you think the meeting went?"

"Great!" He said, "Everyone contributed and we all agreed with the decision!"

He honestly did not notice what I saw. He brain was not conditioned to think inclusively in terms of actual verbal participation from each person in the group.

I also recall how many groups using Mutual Invitation for the first time struggled with the process. In particular, some group members would not remember who had been invited to participate, and needed to ask those who had not spoken to identify themselves. This was an indication that their brains had not yet been trained to think inclusively.

How does Mutual Invitation work in training the brain to become inclusive? To be able to do Mutual Invitation, a person must learn to pay attention to who has been invited and who has not. Over time, the brain expands its ability to notice who is included and who is not. Once developed, this ability extends beyond the times when one is practicing Mutual Invitation; it comes into play in all kind of situations.

The next time you participate in a gathering using Mutual Invitation, pay attention to what you are learning. As you listen to each person and as the conversation moves from person to person, notice who is being invited. Notice and affirm that you and the individuals in the group are learning not just the idea of building inclusive community, but developing a new pattern of thinking inclusively. This pattern of thinking is key to developing our currencies of relationship, truth, and wellness.

17

Holy Conferencing

"Holy conferencing" has been a buzzword term used by the United Methodist Church within the last few years to remind people of the spirit and principles of civil and caring conversations, especially during times of difficult decision-making.

To be *holy* means to follow the likeness of the nature of God instead of that of the world. Therefore, holy conferencing mean setting aside a time and a place to confer with each other in a pattern that follows the divine nature and not the world's. Jesus said:

> You have heard that it was said, "You shall love your neighbor and hate your enemy." But I say to you, Love your enemies and pray for those who persecute you, so that you may be children of your Father in heaven; for he makes his sun rise on the evil and on the good, and sends rain on the righteous and on the unrighteous. For if you love those who love you, what reward do you have?... Be perfect, therefore, as your heavenly Father is perfect. (Matthew 5:43–46a, 48)

To be children of God means to be inclusive, even of our enemies. This radical pattern of inclusion certainly differentiates Christians, when we follow it, from the world's pattern in terms of how we deal with our differences. It is this pattern of radical inclusion that sets us apart and makes us holy. Holy conferencing means setting aside a time and place

- to affirm that we are beloved children of God...
- so we can share our truth...
- and listen to and understand others' truth even when we disagree...
- in order to discover together "our truth."

In the English language, "perfect" often connotes the idea of being flawless. I learned from biblical scholar Walter Wink that in Aramaic, the language that Jesus spoke, the closest word to "perfect" is the word for "complete" or "whole." This makes perfect sense in the reference to the biblical text on "loving your enemy" mentioned earlier. In other words, Jesus tells us to be complete, as God is complete. Be inclusive, as God is inclusive. Be holy, as God is holy.

18

Forward and Backward

Love comes out of God and gathers us to God in order to pour itself back into God through all of us and bring us all back to Him on the tide of His own infinite mercy.[16]

...if you follow Love forward and backward through the circulation from Person to Person, you can never track it to a stop, you can never corner it and hold it down and fix it to one of the Persons as if He could appropriated to Himself the fruit of the love of the others.[17] — Thomas Merton

---

[16]Mihaly Csikszentmihalyi, *Finding Flow* (New York: Basics Book, 1997), 52.
[17]Ibid., 52.

Forward and Backward

(Inspired by Thomas Merton's Seeds of Contemplation)

Accompaniment:

||: C9 /Am7 / Fmaj7 / C9 :||

19

I AM WHO I AM

"Jazz isn't just the music, it's the feeling the music gives you." Bill Strickland wrote this in his inspiring book *Make the Impossible Possible*.

That feeling is the result of an ability to recognize potential in simple things and ordinary situations, then, through improvisation, conviction, and skill, turn that potential into something remarkable... Jazz is a state of mind in which I'm reconnected, with conviction and clarity, to the things that matter most to me. It is a bottomless source of energy and inspiration that reminds me, in simple human terms, why I need to do what I do, and gives me the will and the stamina to keep doing it, despite setbacks and obstacles.[18]

Moses encounters God in the form of a burning bush. According to Exodus 3:2, "The bush was blazing, yet it was not consumed." This is the scene in which God asks Moses to go back to face Pharaoh and to bring the Israelites out of Egypt. However, Moses says to God, "Who am I that I should go to Pharaoh?" God says, "I will be with you." Then Moses asks for God's name, in case he is asked who sent him. God's answer is "I AM WHO I AM"(Exodus 3:9–14).

Moses grew up under the protection of Pharaoh's daughter. One day, he saw an Egyptian beating a Hebrew, one of his own people. Moses struck down the Egyptian and then hid him in the sand. Afraid for his life, he fled Egypt and settled in the land of Midian. By the time he encountered the burning bush, he was living a comfortable life, married with children.

His passion for what was just and right had gotten him into trouble before. His passion, and perhaps even rage, was something that burned and consumed. It consumed his livelihood in Egypt and perhaps it consumed him—losing sight of his call and hiding in Midian as a shepherd. Encountering the burning bush reignited his passion for justice. But this time, the bush was not consumed—God promised Moses that his passion would bring about life for many. His passion, instead of consuming, would take a people to a place where resources would flow—a land of mike and honey. The burning bush was the symbol of his original calling, with which Moses needed to reconnect.

---

[18]Strickland with Rause, *Make the Impossible Possible*, 106–107.

But Moses wanted more certainty. He wanted to know the name of God. God answered him like a jazz master. "I will be with you," God said (and I improvise God's answer further): "Oh, by the way, I AM WHO I AM. You don't need to know any more. As long as you have your passion for justice and I am with you, we can improvise as we go. We will encounter many obstacles, but we will have plenty of energy and innovations to get us through."

People who live the cycle of blessing are like jazz musicians. We share a vision for a sustainable future fed by the cycle of blessings—that is the song structure on which we improvise together, making new songs and finding new possibilities. Bill Strickland had no idea that the tiny center he started in a forgotten margin of Pittsburgh would evolve into a multi-million-dollar corporation providing premier job training and community arts-education, creating sustainable futures for many people who would have otherwise been stuck in an unsustainable cycle of poverty. Because he knew who he was, and knew the song structure of what makes us sustainable, he improvised using his skills and the resources available to create innovations that might seem impossible to others. He found new ways to do more with less. He burned with passion and conviction that does not consume but rather sustains self and others.

Holy currencies/cycle of blessings is the song structure. You just need to know it and live it and improvise with it. In order to do that, you need to know who you are. Who you are is a verb in the present tense. You are now. You are action. You are connecting. You are changing. You are adapting. All the while, you know who you are. You know the song. You improvise. You create a new song. You go to the edge. You come back. You find new ways to harmonize. You find new melodies that may be crazy, but they work, somehow. You are...who you are.

"When they hand you over, do not worry about how you are to speak or what you are to say; for what you are to say will be given to you at that time; for it is not you who speak, but the Spirit of your Father speaking through you." (Matthew 10:19–20)

20

A Dragon Tale

I grew up with dragon stories. Unlike the negative depictions of dragons in European cultures, Chinese dragons are mythical creatures symbolizing many positive things, such as good fortune, strength, and righteousness. Whenever there are festivities such as Chinese New Year, weddings, or birthdays, you will see the symbol of the dragon in our decorations, our clothes, our dances, and our parades.

Here is one of the dragon tales I learned when I was child:

There once was a man who had a reputation for being a lover of dragons. He embroidered dragons on his clothes. He engraved dragons curling up the pillars of his house. He bought stone sculptures of dragons to decorate his garden. One day a real dragon from heaven heard about this dragon lover and decided to pay him a visit. The dragon poked her head through his front door, wrapped her body with the golden scales around the house and stuck her tail through one of the windows. When the dragon lover saw the real dragon, he was terrified. He ran and hid himself, trembling with fear. The real dragon was disappointed that this so-called dragon lover only loved the images of dragons and not the real ones.

In the United States, we say that we love justice, we love democracy, we love equality, and we love freedom. But when real justice, democracy, equality, and freedom actually arrive, will we be frightened? What will it be like, for those of us who realize that equality means we have to share our abundance with others, and that democracy means we have to listen and understand another point of view even when we disagree?

As Christians, we claim that we love God, we claim that we love Jesus, and we pray, "Thy Kingdom come." Yet, if God's kingdom comes today, how would we react? Would we be frightened by the true incarnation of Jesus, who demands that we love our neighbors as ourselves, feed the hungry, cloth the naked, welcome the strangers, visit those in prison, and take care of the sick (Matthew 25:31–46)?

How can we learn to love not only the *ideas* of justice, freedom, democracy, and equality, but also to realize them, recognize them, and welcome them in our lives? How can we not just love the *idea* of Jesus, but also learn to embody Jesus and be part of the incarnation of Christ in our work, family, and community?

21

Closet Castaways

As a Christian of Chinese heritage, it is a struggle to know what to do during the years when Ash Wednesday, the beginning of Lent, coincides with the start of the Lunar New Year. This year, 2015, was one of those years. I recalled a Chinese tradition that helped me make a compromise. Growing up in Hong Kong, as preparation to welcome the new year, we were required to clean our homes from top and bottom and get rid of stuff that we didn't need. So, on Ash Wednesday 2015, the day before the first day of the Lunar New Year, I cleaned my apartment. In the process, I discovered many things in my closet that I didn't remember owning! This got me thinking: How much stuff is in the closets of every household in the United States?

Sendhil Mullainathan and Eldar Shafir, in their book *Scarcity,* call these forgotten items "closet castaways" and they "are so common that space, not money, becomes the scarce commodity. People need to rent out self-storage facilities to house all their stuff. Some estimate that over $12 billion is spent annually on self-storage, three times as much as is spent on music purchases. In fact, the United States has more than two billion square feet allocated to self-storage space."[19]

What would happen if we began to think of these things as resources and invested them back into our communities? A while ago, I was given a tour of the Life Enrichment Center in Dayton, Ohio. Its mission is to work *"in collaboration with area-wide partners to provide life building, life sustaining services to the underserved in the greater Dayton community."*[20] As part of the center's health and wellness program, they have a gym where people can work out, have conversations, and build social and physical wellness. I asked the tour guide, a United Methodist pastor, where the equipment came from. His eyes twinkled and, with a big smile, he said, "It was easy. I made announcements at the local churches and invited people to go through their garages to see if they had any gym equipment that they were not using. In a couple of weeks, we had a fully equipped gym!"

Imagine two billion square feet worth of closet castaways reinvested back into our communities. Once we clean out our giant closet and no longer need the storage space, imagine $12 billion in storage fees being set free to be invested back into our economy!

---

[19]Sendhil Mullainathan and Eldar Shafir, *Scarcity* (New York: Picador, 2013), 77.
[20]See the website of the Life Enrichment Center at http://www.daytonlec.org/.

One of the traditional Lenten disciplines is for Christians to intentionally give up something. I invite you to find ways to reinvest your closet castaways back into your communities to create social, economic, and ecological wellness. Share this idea with your friends and invite them to do the same. Maybe we can start a movement that can slowly convert this massive amount of forgotten static stuff into dynamic useful resources for creating sustainable communities.

> "Do not store up for yourselves treasures on earth, where moth and rust consume and where thieves break in and steal; but store up for yourselves treasures in heaven, where neither moth nor rust consumes and where thieves do not break in and steal. For where your treasure is, there your heart will be also." (Matthew 6:19–21)

22

What Is Normal?

For most of 2012, I lived with constant pain. My doctor said I had a classic case of shingles, which is a skin rash caused by the same virus that causes chickenpox. After a person has chickenpox, this virus remains dormant in the nervous system and is never fully cleared from the body. Under certain circumstances that no one seems to be able to define, the virus reactivates and causes shingles. Besides the unsightly rash, the pain following the path of the affected nerves was constant, and unbearable at times. There were nights when I wished for a magic lotion or a cooling pool of water into which I could immerse myself to heal the rash and stop the pain.

While I was careful not to be around children and pregnant women, I instinctively kept my medical condition from the people with whom I worked. Perhaps there was a deep sense of shame or fear of rejection associated with sickness that affected the skin. I was taking regular doses of painkillers throughout the day (and night) and acted as if I was normal. After about 10 days, my body was beginning to accept the constant pain, as I reached for my pills to relieve the anticipated pain for the next few hours.

In a passing conversation with a friend, I jokingly said that I was addicted to pain pills and then I stopped myself and asked: "Am I?"

While I didn't really think I had become an addict, this experience caused me to reflect on how easily we adapt to things that are not normal; how readily we cover up reality to continue living in denial. It is not normal for our young men and women to be fighting wars 7,000 miles from home. It is not normal for people who work hard to be unable to afford a safe place to live. It is not normal for a small percentage of people to own and control a large percentage of our nation's money and resources, while the majority of people are struggling. It is not normal for private groups to spend millions of dollars on negative television advertising against a political candidate they don't like, while the economy and job creation are among the key issues in these elections. What pain have these conditions caused us? What painkillers have we been taking to keep up our denial?

After about six months, I was able to tell my friends about my medical condition and not be ashamed. I then stopped taking the pain pills, all the while worrying about how my body would react. Would the pain return? But I was willing to face whatever might come, in order to achieve physical health again. I still remembered what it was like to be healthy and not need pills every four hours to be functional.

What will it take for us, as citizen of the United States, to stop our denial? Do any of us remember what it was like when we were not fighting a war? Do any of us remember what it was like when resources were flowing through every segment of our communities? Do any of us remember what it was like when an election was about who would lead our town, city, state, and nation based on their love and care for the people? Who will help us recall what a healthy nation looks like?

> When Jesus saw him lying there and knew that he had been there a long time, he said to him, "Do you want to be made well?" The sick man answered him, "Sir, I have no one to put me into the pool when the water is stirred up; and while I am making my way, someone else steps down ahead of me." Jesus said to him, "Stand up, take your mat and walk." At once the man was made well, and he took up his mat and began to walk. (John 5:6–9)

23

Money and Freedom of Speech

On April 2, 2014, the United States Supreme Court struck down a decades-old cap on the total amount any individual can contribute to political candidates in federal elections on the grounds that limiting contributions violates the First Amendmant guarantee of freedom of speech. I have no problem with rich people wanting to support the candidates of their choice. In fact, they have always done what they wanted with their money and if the law didn't allow it, they would have used their power to get around it anyway. However, I do have a problem with using the First Amendment to justify this change, by equating freedom of speech with spending money.

As I understand it, the First Amendment was added to the U.S. Constitution to protect the powerless so that their voices could still be heard. Doing this is essential to a healthy democracy. If we lose the ability to hear the diverse voices in our society, and allow only the powerful (politically and economically) to amplify their voices, we cease to be a democratic society, but, instead, become an autocratic society controlled by the rich and powerful.

Freedom of speech is not the same as the freedom to spend money however you please. Money (especially when it is spent on buying media time) amplifies speech; and unlimited money has the power to amplify a particular viewpoint so much that other voices can't be heard. The freedom to use money, in this case, becomes an infringement on others' freedom of speech. In holy currencies language, this would be described as using money to stop the flow of the currency of truth. We don't have the whole truth unless we are able to hear the "still small voices" within our society. A democratic nation must pay attention and find ways to restore its ability to listen to essential and diverse voices in its society.

To take the First Amendment, which was written to protect the poor and powerless, and turn it around to reinforce the power and influence of those who are already powerful contradicts the spirit of the First Amendment and the U. S. Constitution.

> And, behold, the Lord passed by, and a great and strong wind rent the mountains, and brake in pieces the rocks before the Lord; but the Lord was not in the wind: and after the wind an earthquake; but the Lord was not in the earthquake: And after the earthquake a fire; but the Lord was not in the fire: and after the fire a still small voice. (1 Kings 19:11b–12, KJV)

44

24

Awakened Ear—Sustaining Word

As a preacher, I pray that I may preach a word that will sustain those who hear it. I pray that the words I use will inspire others to act in ways that will sustain themselves, their families and friends, their communities, and the earth. It is a lofty goal to set for myself each time I preach. Therefore, I always feel inadequate whenever I approach the awesome task of interpreting the Word. How will the Word connect with people's lives this week? How will my words, working with the Word, enable the spirit to flow, bringing sustenance to the people?

The words I use during the 10 to 20 minutes of sermon time are only half of the event. It is like breathing; speaking is "breathing-out," and listening is "breathing-in" that sustains me as a preacher. Each time I prepare to preach, I remind myself to awaken my ears to listen to my own heart, to the people in the community, to what is happening in society, and to what is happening on the earth on which I stand. Awakening my ears requires me to see and hear what *is*, and not what I think things should be. It is about truly noticing what is happening around me without applying my own interpretation or judgment. I must awaken my ears to listen to the cry of the broken-hearted, the mourning of the weary, the sighing of the wounded, the unspoken insecurity of the rich, the silent protest of the poor, the innocence of the uncertain questioners, the scheme of the selfish, the hope of the desperate, and the groaning of creation.

We develop our currency of truth by awakening our ears to hear the voices behind and around the loud and overpowering noise of the powerful ones who control and define what they want us to believe is the truth. By listening to these small, quiet voices—of our fellow human beings, and of the Spirit—we can speak and sustain the weary with a word of Truth.

> The Lord God has given me
>   the tongue of a teacher,
> that I may know how to sustain
>   the weary with a word.
> Morning by morning God wakens--
>   wakens my ear
>   to listen as those who are taught. (Isaiah 50:4)

25

Sustain the Weary with a Word

(Dedicated to the families and friends of those who died in the Sandy Hook Elementary School shooting in Newtown, Connecticut, on December 14, 2012.)

Sustain the weary with a word
A word of grace to hold the broken
A word so deep and wide, it can't be spoken
Sustain the weary with a word of grace.
Sustain the weary with a word
A word of truth with no denying
The thund'rous roar of pain and silent crying
Sustain the weary with a word of truth.
Sustain the weary with a word
A word of peace in spite of warring
Emotions claiming hopes of life restoring.
Sustain the weary with a word of peace.
Sustain the weary with a word
A word of love to pierce the numbness
And reach for common pain that speaks of oneness.
Sustain the weary with a word of love.

Sustain the Weary with a Word

Sust-ain the wea-ry___ with a word___ A word of
A word of
A word of
A word of

grace_____ to hold the brok - en___ a word so
truth_____ with no de - ny - ing___ the thun-derous
peace_____ in spite of war - ring___ e - mo - tions
love_____ to pierce the numb-ness___ and reach for

deep and___ wide it can't be spok-en___ Sus-tain the
roar of___ pain and si - lent cry - ing___ Sus - tain the
claim - ing___hopes of life re - stor-ing___ Sus - tain the
com - mon pain that speaks of one - ness___ Sus - tain the

wea - ry____ with a word of____ grace.
wea - ry____ with a word of____ truth.
wea - ry____ with a word of____ peace.
wea - ry____ with a word of____ love.

26

Pledge Card for Currency of Truth

The currency of truth is the ability to articulate, individually and corporately, the global and holistic truth. The internal dimension of the currency of truth encompasses the experiences of different individuals and groups within the church or ministry. The external dimension comes from the experiences of different individuals and groups in the community, neighborhood, city, town, nation, and earth.[21] Lent is a good time to invite your fellow church members to make a commitment to discerning the truth. This pledge card prompts members to value the importance of truth—for themselves, their church, their neighborhood, their country and the earth. The commitment to discern truth about myself and my family may include things such as learning why I or my family consistently behave in a certain way, discerning my call to ministry, doing some family history work, or listening to the quiet ones in my family. The other commitments to discern the truth may include creating a "truth event" around the issues that the church faces internally or externally. A truth event may involve having church members and people in the neighborhood come together for a constructive dialogue on an important issue such as police and community relations, interracial conflict, economic disparity, housing concerns, conserving water and other natural resources, or cleaning up the environment.

The currency of truth flows naturally into wellness and relationship. Truth strengthens relationships internally and externally. Truth challenges members of the church to invest their time, place, money, and gracious leadership to address the discerned issues, moving communities toward greater wellness. Fill out this pledge card and find an Accountable Person to witness and sign it. Submit the card to your church leaders. If they don't know what it is, take the opportunity to start a conversation about the importance of truth as a currency.

---

[21]See full description of the currency of truth in Eric H. F. Law, *Holy Currencies* (St. Louis: Chalice Press, 2013), 43–59.

Pledge Card for Currency of Truth

- I commit to discover/discern the truth about _____ for myself and/or my family.
- I commit to discern the truth about _____ in my church.
- I commit to discern the truth about _____ in my neighborhood, my town/city, or my country.
- I commit to discern the truth about _____ about the earth.

My name: _____ My accountable person: _____

_____   _____
        signature   signature

Date: _____

27

A Fig Tree in the Vineyard

"A man had a fig tree planted in his vineyard; and he came looking for fruit on it and found none. So he said to the gardener, 'See here! For three years I have come looking for fruit on this fig tree, and still I find none. Cut it down! Why should it be wasting the soil?' He replied, 'Sir, let it alone for one more year, until I dig around it and put manure on it. If it bears fruit next year, well and good; but if not, you can cut it down.'" (Luke 13:6–9)

Jesus told this story as a response to questions about misfortune, punishment, and sin. Most people interpreted the parable this way: The "man" is God. We are the fig tree. God is not pleased that we don't bear fruit, and threatens to destroy us. The gardener is Jesus, who pleads on our behalf and buys us some time—a grace period to get our act together.

I subscribed to this interpretation until I studied this text with a group of Chinese refugees from Southeast Asia. After listening to the story, one of the participants asked, "What's a fig tree doing in a vineyard?" This question opened my eyes to new dimensions of this story I had never thought of before.

"What kind of fruit is this man looking for?" He continued his inquiry. "If he is looking for grapes, he isn't going to find any. Besides, the Chinese name of fig is 'no-flower fruit'; so a fig tree bears fruit differently from the grapevines." As we explored further on this theme, another participant said, "Back in Vietnam, I was a doctor; now I wash dishes in a restaurant. People in America don't see the fruit we bear."

We often think of a "grace period" as a little more time to do what we have to do to get by. In 2013, we witnessed the U.S. Congress procrastinating during a grace period over the so-called "fiscal cliff" and "sequester cuts." Instead of using the grace period to understand the issues in new ways and see them from different perspectives, our nation's leaders simply reinforced their static beliefs during this time. In other words, they were saying the same old thing: we want "fruit" as we define it. They used the grace period as a time for additional political maneuvering designed to gain the upper hand.

Perhaps it is time to see the fig tree for what it is, and not expect it to grow and bear fruit like grapevines. Perhaps we need to use the grace period to listen to those who are impacted in local communities, like the fig trees in the parable, and appreciate the gifts and talents they bring to the nation. In the Exodus story, God had "observed the misery of my people who are in Egypt" and "heard their cry." (Exodus 3:7) God, with the help of Moses, solved the slavery problem with an innovative solution: liberate the captives. When we are able to see an issue from the perspective of those who suffer, we may discover innovative solutions to our problems.

28

Truth and Grace at the Margin

In 2013, I boarded a bus with 25 religious leaders at BorderLinks in Tucson, Arizona. According to its website, BorderLinks "envisions a world in which people, within and across social borders, respect and care for each other, value and celebrate differences, and build healthy and just communities where everyone has equal opportunity for a full and dignified life."

The organization has a powerful mission:

Through dynamic educational experiences, BorderLinks connects divided communities, raises awareness about the impact of border and immigration policies, and inspires action for social transformation.[22]

The BorderLinks bus took our group toward the U.S./Mexico border at Nogales, which "was once an easy, friendly and relaxed two-nation border town" as described in the official website of Nogales, Arizona. "The urban fabric is now split in two," the website description continues. Part of Nogales lies in the U.S. and part in Mexico; some call the combined city Ambos Nogales. (*Ambos* means "both" in Spanish.) Although a heavily patrolled international border now divides the city, citizens and businesses on both sides still rely on each other, the website explains.

This somewhat neutral description quickly evaporated as we moved close enough to the dividing wall to look over to the Mexico side of Nogales. While the website's description of the U.S. portion of Nogales as "a progressive city that has been able to maintain its small town charm, rich traditions, and vibrant culture" seemed accurate, on the Mexico side, we saw dwellings made of unfinished cinderblocks, car tires, and wood panels, crowded together on the hillside and seeming to push up against the border wall.

After we crossed into Nogales, Sonora, we listened to stories of people who were planning on crossing the border illegally in order to be with families and make a better living. Some had repeatedly been deported back from the U.S. and were determined to try again.

We drove by the manufacturing plants called *maquiladoras,* which took advantage of proximity to the U.S. and the abundance of cheap labor in order to maximize profit. We had lunch in a cinderblock house, where our

---

[22]See BorderLinks' website at https://www.borderlinks.org/.

gracious host told us about her struggles to challenge the factories to honor the rights of the workers, who made an average wage equivalent to $35 to $75 per week.

As we continued our journey, I saw a vision in my mind of a large machine. People were forced into walking restricted paths to be devoured by this machine. Even while fighting the system, they were still confined by the rules of the machine. As I looked around, I was desperate to find hope.

Finally, we arrived at the Hogar de Esperanza y Paz (Home of Hope and Peace, also known as HEPAC), where the organizers were finally sharing stories of hope. HEPAC offers adult education programs, programs for children, community gardens, and micro-economic development. These programs create reasons for people to stay in Mexico.

This place of grace seemed so small in the face of the enormous and destructive system of cross-border exchanges that favor wealthy corporations and individuals, while the poor struggle to find sustainability in ways that include making the desperate and dangerous journey north. Yet this glimpse of hope is what we have to hold on to. As long as there are systems that exploit poor people, we will always have the poor among us. And we might try to help the poor within this system, but our limited effort is not going to address the root cause of the problem. The solution is to transform the system, or at least name and imagine an alternative sustainable community. We begin with connecting with organizations such as BorderLinks that tell the truth and show us a little grace at the margin. Equipped with the currency of truth, we then share and expand it using our currencies of relationships, inviting more people to invest their time to make the journey to the border to experience the truth. When more people know the truth, which steers them toward investing their resources to foster wellness of the poor and oppressed, we will have a better chance to truly transform our systems from scarcity to abundance, from limiting border to expanding margin, and from fear to grace.

29

Danger of Disconnect

The Los Angeles riots happened on April 29, 1992. I was living in L.A. at that time, and I remember the nonstop media coverage. I also recall the sight (the smoke in the sky), the sound (the sirens of the police cars and fire trucks) and the smell (burning plastic) of that day and the days that followed. I remember most vividly feeling torn between empathy toward those who were angry with injustice, and dismay at the disturbing and destructive behaviors.

In retrospect, the underlying cause was an unsustainable community. In the United States, we are taught that all are equal and each individual has inalienable rights to life, liberty, and the pursuit of happiness. But for many who are trying to survive in unsustainable communities, where resources are not flowing, we hear the immediate rebuke: *BUT NOT FOR ME.* I could hear in my head people saying, "Look, we got solid proof this time—the videotape of the beating of Rodney King by the four policemen—and yet we still don't have justice! The system acquitted them!" The anger, for many, translated into, "Let's take what we can get now because we will never get our share no matter how hard we try."

The fact that the destruction and looting were carried out by people who lived in the same neighborhoods indicates that people were not connected. If they had had real relationships with their neighbors, they would not have been stealing and destroying their property. Not only were they not connected with one another, they were not connected to the spirituality of abundance—if we share what we have, there will be enough to feed everyone, to shelter everyone, and to enable everyone to live a productive and happy life. By not being connected, they were like branches cut from the vine—dried up and ready to burn when ignited by the spark of anger.

As I examine the similarities between the L.A. riots of 1992 and the events of 2014 and 2015 that (again) raised issues of race to a boiling point, I am reminded of the danger of disconnect—a deficiency of the currency of relationship. Our work and ministry must include the creation and nurture of networks, locally and globally, so that people are connected through love, compassion, and mutual respect. By redeveloping the currency of relationship, we tap into the flow of abundant sources for life, creating times and places in which we can speak truth to each other and to the system, and can foster social, economic, spiritual, and ecological wellness.

Relational Events

Invite members of your community to gather and explore ways to develop currency of relationship:

- Ask participants to think about what they can do to create events (a time and a place) where people in their community can establish respectful relationships between residents, families, businesses, religious groups, and civic organizations. Ideas could include a neighborhood celebration, a community film festival with discussion, a police-community dialogue, a work day to beautify the neighborhood, an emergency preparedness seminar, or a health fair.

- As a group, select three of the participants' ideas. Then divide into three small groups. Each group takes one of the ideas, works out the details, and creates an action plan for the event.

- Ask each group to report on what they accomplished.

- Now invite participants to consider: As result of this exploration what am I called to do?

30

Embrace the Darkness

When Christians celebrate Holy Week, we retell or even reenact the tragedy of a man named Jesus of Nazareth. The drama begins with the people waving palm branches and singing praises to welcome Jesus to Jerusalem, as they express hope that he might be the long-awaited savior. But Jesus' words and actions reveal a different way of understanding God. He believes that we are all sons and daughters of God and, therefore, all equal and connected. We are to treat each other as if we are part of the same body in everything we do. If one of us is hurt, all of us hurt. If one of us is oppressed, we all suffer.

Because of his actions firmly grounded in this vision, Jesus is betrayed by one of his best friends, abandoned by most of them—except for a few women and his mother—and, finally, sentenced to death by the same people who welcomed him enthusiastically at the beginning of the story. The drama takes us to the bitter end, when he was executed like a common criminal.

Why do Christians want to relive a story with such an unhappy ending every year? The Holy Week drama reminds us of the woeful side of human community. We might embrace the idea of something new at first, but when we find out it is not what we assumed, we reject it.

For example, we like the idea that all are created as equal. It is written in the *Declaration of Independence*. But for some, if this means giving up or sharing what we have, the idea is not so great after all. As a result, we have a system in which some groups are more equal than others. For more than 200 years, people in the United States have been struggling with the tension between wanting to make true equality a reality, and rejecting it out of fear. From various amendments to the *Constitution* to the Congressional debate over the federal budget and the possibility of a government shutdown, these struggles are part of the drama of living into the idea that all people should be equal. As Christians move toward Easter, we allow the drama of Jesus, his friends, and his betrayers remind us of how we are to act. Do we act out of our fear, or do we act out of the conviction of our vision? We have a choice in how our own drama unfolds.

At one point during Holy Week, either at the end of Passion Sunday or Good Friday worship, we are left with Jesus dead in the tomb, and the disciples feeling hopeless. But this is not the end of the story. The story will continue. It has to continue.

We must take a holistic view of this event, including what goes on before and after, in order to know the truth of the whole story. Night and day, sleep and wake, darkness and light are all part of the rhythm of life. Winter and spring are parts of the seasons. "Turning the other cheek" is part of confronting your enemy and connecting with him or her as a fellow human being. Nonviolent protest met with violent retaliation is part of the process that exposes the injustice and oppression of our system. Death and resurrection are parts of the cycle of living. Our human instinct is to avoid the hurt, the betrayal, and the unknown. However, we must embrace the darkness, knowing the cycle will come around and there will be light. While we wait, we listen to each other with awakened ears. While we wait, we speak the words that sustain each other.

31

Those Who Sowed with Tears

Those who sowed with tears will reap with songs of joy.
Those who go out weeping, carrying the seed,
Will come again with joy, will come again with joy,
Shouldering the sheaves. *(based on Psalm 126:6–7)*

Those Who Sowed with Tears

Psalm 126:6–7
Principal Canon

Salmo 126:6
Español

Los que sem-bra-ron_ con lá - gri- mas, co-se-cha-
ron con gri-tos_ de a-le-grí - a. Los que sem-bra-ron_ con
lá - gri- mas, co-se-cha-ron con gri-tos__ de a-le - gría.___

詩篇 126:6 (中文)
Psalm 126:6 in Chinese

那 些 流 淚 撒 種 的 人
必 將 會 歡 會。 歡 呼 收 割. 那 些 流
淚 撒 種 的 人 必 將 會 歡 呼 收 割。

Although originally composed for Cantonese, this may be sung using the Mandarin pronunciation.

English-Language Descant
Psalm 126:6

Those who sowed with tears_____ will reap with

songs of joy._____ Those who sowed with

tears_____ will reap with songs of joy._____

Accompaniment

32

Chance or Planned?

One Friday in April of 2012, people from 44 states in the U.S. spent nearly $1.5 billion on Mega Millions lottery tickets. This is equivalent to nearly $5 for every man, woman, and child in the country. In Maryland alone, a record $11.8 million was spent on lottery tickets that Friday. In some locations where lottery tickets were sold, people waited for up to three hours in lines that wrapped around the block. Each person who bought a ticket dreamed of winning the jackpot of $640 million. But each ticket had only a one-in-176 million chance of winning.

About a month earlier, in Sanford, Florida, 17-year-old Trayvon Martin, an African American, was walking from a convenience store to the home of his father's girlfriend. He was shot and killed by 28-year-old George Zimmerman, a man of mixed ethnicity (Peruvian and Anglo American). Zimmerman was a neighborhood watch coordinator. He was arrested and questioned by police, and then released without charges.

Through the network of social media, this little-known incident gained national attention, precipitating the "Million Hoodies March" in New York City's Union Square on March 21. More than 2 million people demanded Zimmerman's arrest via a Change.org petition started by Trayvon Martin's mother. By March 30, the day of the Mega Million Mania, CNN and all the major news networks were running the story of Trayvon Martin and George Zimmerman.

These seemingly unrelated events illustrate two ways of mobilizing resources. One has to do with the flow of billions of dollars converging at liquor stores, convenience stores, and newsstands for a slim chance of financial return. The other has to do with the flow of information and relationships energized by a passion for justice and truth for one young man walking home from a convenience store. The first depended on chance, with the vast majority disappointed on Monday; the other was constructed to result in concrete actions for justice and truth—the arrest of Zimmerman and the reopening of the case.

These two events demonstrate that there is an abundance of resources—relationship, truth, and money. We just need a plan to mobilize them. What if we combined incentive for people to come up with $1.5 billion a day with the networking ability fueled by a passion for truth and wellness within our communities? How many jobs could we create? How many homes could we save from foreclosure? How many scholarships could we offer young men and women for education? How many job-training centers could we establish?

How many community gardens could we plant? How many homes could we power with clean energy? How many community organizations could we create to sustain the people in our communities socially, physically, and spiritually?

Don't leave the use of your resources to chance. The children of Israel did not leave slavery in Egypt by chance; they planned their exodus toward freedom with God through Moses. Jesus did not die on the cross on Good Friday by chance; he planned it with God so that his followers would learn what it meant to be children of God on Easter Day. Plan how you use your resources through networking with others, investing them into the flow of resources that will sustain you, your family, and your community.

Passion and Resources

Invite members of your community to gather and explore the connections between their passion and resources:

- Invite participants to offer up to $20 and put the money in a basket.
- Count up the resulting amount of money and put that number on a wall chart.
- Have participants form small groups and explore what they can do with that amount of money for the benefit of their community.
- Ask each group to share their ideas.
- Invite participants to consider how they can network with others to further support some of the ideas that emerged in this dialogue.
- Conclude by gathering with participants and inviting them to complete the sentences:

  - I notice...
  - I wonder...

33

Path of Life

It was Holy Saturday, the day before Easter, in 2011. I was in New York City feeling trapped in my family's apartment as the cold rain poured down outside. In fact, it had been cold and rainy for most of Holy Week. As I practiced what I wrote—to embrace the darkness and stay in "the empty tomb," I felt that death, like winter, had such a strong grip on the world that it was overwhelming my own movement toward Easter.

Easter is just one day, is what went through my mind. *The world is the same before Easter. The world is still the same after Easter. There is no resolution in the unrest in Libya. We are still losing lives in the wars in Iraq and Afghanistan. The crisis in Japan is still a crisis. We are not finished with the aftermath of the oil spills in the Gulf, the earthquake in Haiti, the hurricane in New Orleans, and all the other disasters around the globe. Healthcare costs are still going up. Gas prices are remaining at over $4 per gallon. The rich are still getting richer, and the poor stay poor.*

As I wrapped myself in a blanket and watched the rain fall outside my window, the nagging question echoed in my head: Easter is almost here, but has anything changed? As I wallowed in the darkness, I remembered a book I had bought (yes, I still buy books) during a visit to the Museum of Modern Art (MOMA) titled *WorldChanging: A User's Guide for the 21st Century.* In the introduction, Bill McKibben, founder of 350.org (a global grassroots movement to solve the climate crisis) wrote:

> I can remember what it was like to give an Earth Day talk twenty years ago—you needed to keep your fingers firmly crossed, and hope. You could conjure up a rough image of, say, a solar-powered world, but a rough image was all it was... Describing a bright green future took a strong imagination.[23]

He went on to describe how things have changed today. Many of the innovations that he talked about 20 years ago are now reality. But there is still much to do, especially when climate change has shown little sign of changing course. He proposed:

> [O]ur job is to speed the transition to the other world these innovations promise—to make them not wonderful exceptions,

---

[23]*WorldChanging: A User's Guide for the 21st Century,* ed. Alex Steffen (New York: Abrams, 2011), 13.

but the rule. And doing that will be difficult, because the old world doesn't die away easily.[24]

Ah, "the old world doesn't die away easily"; that was what I was feeling during Holy Week that year. As I read McKibben's book, I recalled the signs of hope—things had indeed changed and were changing—especially concerning the subject about which McKibben was passionate. For example, I had picked up the book *WorldChanging* from a whole island of books with similar topics—sustainable design, art, and architecture prominently placed in the middle of the MOMA store. On a train coming back from Princeton, I had seen solar-powered street lamps through a whole section of a town. Walking around the Bowery, the neighborhood where I grew up, I discovered a Green Depot store selling green products and building materials. In the tourist-filled streets of the SOHO neighborhood, I found a store call *Sprout* that sells eco-friendly watches at reasonable prices. The company claimed that its watches were 80 percent eco-friendly, boasting materials such as organic cotton, mineral crystal, and mercury-free batteries.

I was visiting my nephew's business *Vision Essential*, in Astoria, Queens. As I was helping my friend pick out a frame for his glasses, I was delighted to find a line of frames called Eco Conscious Optics (ECO), made from recycled stainless steel and acetate. For every frame bought, the company would plant a tree. And the prices were about half the cost of other designer frames. Of course, I recommended them to my friend and he bought one.

As I recalled these things, I convinced myself that there was a movement forward in spite of setbacks.

So what would change when Easter arrived tomorrow? The world might stay more or less the same, before and after Easter. What had changed was the choice I made. What had been transformed was my mindset. I could choose to wallow in the paralysis of a seemingly unsustainable personal life, community, nation, and world, or I could choose to act in ways that joined in the movement for a sustainable future. I could be overwhelmed by death, or I could choose the path of life. Sometimes we might not readily see this path, but we must pay attentions to the signs all around us, like spring waiting behind the wintery rain, ready to spring forth.

Just as the story of Easter continues and the disciples struggle with post-Easter fear and doubt before coming to believe, live, and act as a resurrected people, we, too, are invited to shift our mindset and join in the path of life, where our hope for a grace-filled and sustainable future is imperishable, undefiled, and unfading.

---

[24]Ibid., 15.

Signs of Hope

Invite members of your community to spend this week noticing the signs of hope and sustainability in your community/neighborhood.

1. Gather people from your community and invite them to share what they observed and make a list of the "signs."
2. Invite them to consider these questions: What are the elements that make up these signs of sustainability? How can we connect these signs to build a stronger movement toward sustainability for our community?

34

Easter

Easter[25]
Children in white, pink and yellow
Stuffed bunnies from supermarkets
Baskets with sparkling cellophane
Chocolate candies in the shapes of rabbits
Colorful eggs hidden behind bushes
Easter
Birds singing
Flowers blooming
Trees budding
Sun warming faces
Fragrances of spring
Easter
A man, a teacher
A friend of the outcasts, poor, unclean, and powerless
He healed the broken
He acted in love
He was hope
A light in darkness
Easter
A man
Falsely accused, condemned, suffered, died
Three days later
His friends discovered his body gone
They went in the tomb
Saw the linen wrappings lying
Puzzled, confused
They left
Went home
Easter
A woman
Remained by the empty tomb
She stayed and wept
She stayed and saw the angels

---

[25]See the video at http://www.youtube.com/user/GraceInCyberspace?feature=m
hum#p/u/3/lP_Ia0Zitdg).

She stayed and asked questions
She stayed long enough to meet her friend and teacher again
Alive!
Easter
Willingness to stay by the empty tomb
Uncomfortable, confused, unpleasant
But stay
Don't avoid the darkness
Stay to grieve your loss
Don't dismiss the empty tomb
Stay to ask questions
Don't run away from the discomfort
Stay long enough to encounter the risen Christ
New light
New hope
New energy
New directions

35

A New Heart I'll Give to You

A new heart I'll give to you.
A new spirit I will put within you,
And I'll take out of your flesh the heart of stone
And give you a heart of flesh.
I will sprinkle fresh clean water upon you.
From all your idols I will cleanse you
And you shall be my people
And I shall be your God.
Thus says your God.
(Paraphrase, Ezekiel 36:25–28)

A New Heart I'll Give to You

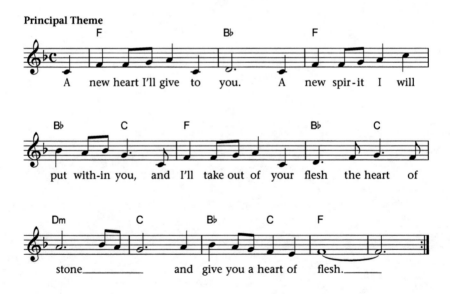

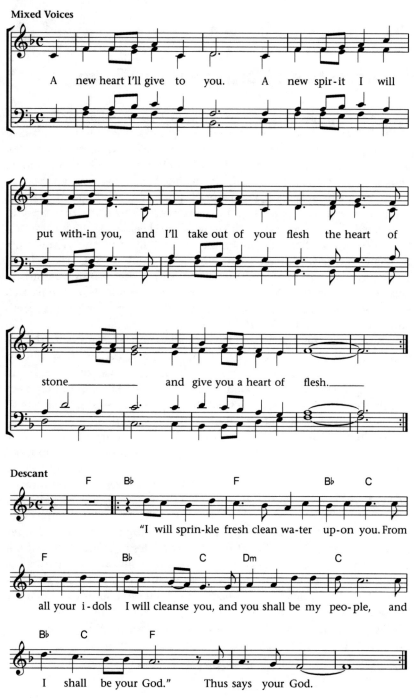

Mixed Voices

A new heart I'll give to you. A new spir-it I will put with-in you, and I'll take out of your flesh the heart of stone_____ and give you a heart of flesh._____

Descant

"I will sprin-kle fresh clean wa-ter up-on you. From all your i-dols I will cleanse you, and you shall be my peo-ple, and I shall be your God." Thus says your God.

36

Resurrection: Vampires and Jesus

While preparing for a weekend video-making workshop for the youth of the Episcopal Diocese of Los Angeles, I jokingly said, "If we don't give them a specific topic, they would most likely make a vampire movie." So, in order to ensure that the young people didn't make vampire or zombie videos, we gave each team a psalm on which to base the videos they created.

Upon further reflection, young people today probably know more about vampirism than Christianity! I did a little research on the Internet and discovered the following: Over 300 movies have been made about vampires, and over 160 of them featured Dracula, making him one of the most frequently portrayed characters in film, second only to Sherlock Holmes. There have been more than 20 television shows that feature vampirism. Over 1,000 vampire novels have been published, most within the past 25 years. When I typed the words "vampire" and "resurrection" into a search engine together, I got over 7 million results.

In contrast, there have been fewer than 40 movies made about the life of Jesus. At the time I wrote this, only a handful of television shows offered by the mainstream media had featured Jesus. Of course, there are many books about Jesus; the most popular of which is the Bible. But in terms of popularity, Jesus doesn't seem to measure up to vampires, even though both the Jesus story and the vampire myth feature resurrection.

During the Easter season, Christians need to reclaim and tell the story of the life-sustaining resurrection of Jesus. Vampires' resurrections are about the continuation and spread of death. Jesus' resurrection is about giving life to all who believe. Vampires return to their coffins every day and walk by night eternally. Jesus left the tomb on Easter Day forever, and he challenges believers to arrive at a new understanding of eternal life—to live in the light, in spite of death. Vampires heal rapidly, presenting a beautiful, seductive façade to cover up the reality of pain and scars. Jesus' resurrection did not erase the wounds from his crucifixion. Vampires consume human blood, draining life. When they bite others, more are turned into bloodthirsty, life-depleting beings. Jesus offers his body and blood symbolically through the blessings of wine and bread, so that those who share in them will continue his life-giving ministry. Jesus' resurrection inspired his followers to share everything they owned, creating sustainable communities.

The unsustainability of our economy during the beginning of the 21st century was vampire-based. Every time a bank approved a loan, that bank received income. The greater the number and amount of loans granted, the more money a bank received from people's down payments—their hard-earned money. So, by giving more loans to people, particularly those who could not afford these loans, banks continued to suck money out of their customers without regard for the well-being of these customers. The banks were acting like vampires. Then, when the economy tanked, the U.S. government, instead of bailing out the people—the blood-drained victims—bailed out the banks! The vampires continued to be in control—no life-sustaining resurrection was offered for the people.

On a personal level, a student of mine asked me, "How do you know you have a good relationship?" My response: "I know that when I am in a bad relationship, I feel drained and tired by being with that person. So a good relationship should be energizing and regenerative. Being in a good relationship gives me the security to give of myself generously without fear. Having this relationship allows me to do more with less." I was talking about the kind of relationship modeled after Jesus' resurrection.

Many people get into vampire-like personal relationships, thinking these are normal, even when they are destructive, addictive, energy-depleting, spiritually draining. Perhaps this happens because they have been conditioned to romanticize the vampire-victim relationship. There is a difference between losing yourself (the vampire way) and giving yourself for another out of love of others, self, and God (the Jesus way).

The fact that people know more about vampirism than Christianity is not a bad thing. It can provide an opportunity for us to explain Jesus' life-sustaining resurrection by contrasting the difference. Especially during the Easter season, start a conversation with someone about the difference between the resurrection of Jesus and vampires. The currency of truth can be exchanged here for increased understanding of our destructive relationships and our unsustainable economy. The truth can set us free to explore other life-giving ways to transform both our relationships and our economy.

> Jesus said to her, "I am the resurrection and the life. Those who believe in me, even though they die, will live, and everyone who lives and believes in me will never die. Do you believe this?" (John 11:25–26)

Vampire

Invite members of your community to explore "vampire" as a symbol of unsustainability:

- Ask participants to brainstorm a list of characteristics of vampires based on their knowledge from books, movies and other media.
- Have participants form small groups. Each group is given one of the following topics:
- Personal Relationships
- Economy
- Environment
- Community Resources
- Invite each group to explore how the characteristics of vampires can be applied to the current state of their topic.
- Ask each small group to report.
- Invite participants to consider alternative images/characters for a sustainable personal relationship economy environment and community.
- Ask participants to consider the question: As a result of today's dialogue what am I called to do?

37

Have Much But Not Too Much

As it is written,
"The one who had much did not have too much,
and the one who had little did not have too little."
(2 Crinthians 8:15)

This was the advice that Paul gave to the first Christian community in Corinth some 2,000 years ago.

In 2,000 years, human beings have not changed much when it comes to giving. Paul was dealing with hesitation and fear fostered by the reigning spirituality of scarcity. He wrote, "I do not mean that there should be relief for others and pressure on you, but it is a question of a fair balance between your present abundance and their need, so that their abundance may be for your need, in order that there may be a fair balance" (2 Corinthians 8:13–14. Then he quoted from the Hebrew scriptures the line with which I opened this reflection, referring to the story of Hebrew people in the wilderness. When they were hungry, God gave them manna from heaven, along with instructions for each to collect what they needed and no more (Exodus 16:15b–18).

The assumption behind Paul's advice was that the way resources were distributed was not fair or balanced. The solution to restoring balance was for those who had a lot to give to those in need. Notice that Paul immediately addresses their fear by saying "so that their abundance may be for your need" in return. That is, if you give, you get back.

This reciprocal idea about giving is holy currency/cycle of blessings thinking. The act of giving activates the circulation of resources, as opposed to holding onto what we have, which stops the flow of resources. If we stop thinking about giving as a one-time linear process and understand it as circulatory, we begin to notice how things start to move and flow in gracious directions. In good time, we receive again. What we receive might not be exactly what we gave, but the gifts are enriching nonetheless.

How do you help your community to actively realize the vision, "The one who has much does not have too much, and the one who has little does not have too little."

For you know the generous act of our Lord Jesus Christ, that though he was rich, yet for your sakes he became poor, so that by his poverty you might become rich. (2 Corinthians 8:9)

73

38

Gift Economy

GracEconomics is a gift-based system of holy currency exchanges that ensures the ongoing circulation of currencies to cultivate a sustainable ministry. Applying GracEconomics to the flow of money in an entrepreneurial ministry usually means providing a range in which a client or guest can contribute. If the client or guest does not have money, he or she can pay with other currencies, such as time, relationship, talent, truth, or gracious leadership.

"How much does it cost to have you come to do a workshop?" This is a typical question my clients ask. This question is based on a commodity economy, which views me and my resources as something that can be bought with money. In other words, I am being valued by money.

Here is my GracEconomic response, "Between $0 and $3,000 per eight-hour day. We ask our clients to contribute as close to the top end of the range as they are able, so that we can provide our resources to groups that have little to no financial resources." This answer adds a new dimension to the exchange—that of a gift economy. Yes, I am willing to do this for free as a gift. But if you have to value my time and expertise with money, $3,000 is about right. The conversation after my response often moves to: Is this important to do? If it is worth doing, then let's work out the appropriate exchanges, which may or may not involve money. The conversation moved from, "Can I buy this?" to, "Let's be friends and work this out with the right exchanges."

Lewis Hyde, in his classic book *The Gift,* makes distinctions between a gift economy and a commodity economy. In a commodity economy, a person's worth is measured by how much he or she owns and keeps. In a gift economy, a person's worth is measured by how much that person gives away. The exchange of a gift establishes relationship between the giver and the receiver. In a commodity economy, using money to valuate the product puts a distance between the trading parties; the transaction can be between strangers. By contrast, the exchange of gifts presumes the parties involved are friends. The giving of gifts abolishes the boundary between the parties, while the commodity economy establishes and maintains the boundaries.

In a gift economy, the receiver of the gift is expected to give it away. The gift remains in circulation throughout the community. In a commodity economy, the exchange is one-way and the product is removed from circulation and often consumed by the new owner. When a *gift* is money, there is no expectation of a return with interest. In a commodity exchange, money is loaned out and expected to return with interest. Gift economy moves resources toward the empty—from the have to the have-not. Commodity economy moves resources toward the profit-making party, often at the expense of the poor.

A gift can be an agent for change and transformation and is the bearer of new life. Commodity economy maintains the system of exchanges with rules that reinforce the status quo. Gift economy is abundance-based. Commodity economy is scarcity based.[26]

A few years ago, I was working on a proposal that involved a three-year relationship with a group of churches. The judicatory leader assured me that the organization had money and he had given me a ballpark figure that the organization had set aside for this project. In a moment of weakness, I submitted a proposal without GracEconomics. That is, instead of giving the client a GracEconomic range, I quoted him a fixed price. Three months later, I received an e-mail that said the decision-making body had debated this proposal and decided not to fund it. There was no explanation of why they turned the proposal down. I wrote back thanking the judicatory leader for his time and I did not get a reply. A few months later, I was at a conference at which this judicatory leader was present. In passing, he said he would talk to me about what happened, but never followed up.

In retrospect, by simply submitting a proposal requesting a fixed amount of funding, I had fallen into the trap of commodity economics. It created a boundary between myself, the client, and the decision-making body he represented. All they needed to do was approve the proposal with money requested, or not. There was no potential for further dialogue to explore their goals, and how my organization could assist them in other ways. The commodity economic process put a distance between us and we became strangers, and this fragile relationship could be cut off at any time without obligation.

In another situation, I began a covenanted relationship with an Episcopal Diocese which accepted a GracEconomic proposal I had submitted. Three years later, we are entering into another agreement approved by the Bishop and the Diocesan Council. The vision was to move the majority of congregations and ministries toward missional thinking and action within the next few years. The bishop called me in the middle of the negotiation and said, "We are getting really excited about this movement. They really like you and trusted you when you spoke to us at our convention. Oh, by the way, don't worry about the money, we will pay at least the middle of the range if not higher once we get the financial piece done."

---

[26]See Lewis Hyde, *The Gift* (New York: Vintage Books, 2007), 3–31.

I have been practicing the gift-based GracEconomics for a number of years since the founding of the Kaleidoscope Institute. Financially, the institute had been fine and we continue to grow steadily. More importantly, by infusing gift economics into our exchanges, we gain so much more in the currencies of relationship and truth.

39

Right Side of the Boat

A pastor who had participated in a Holy Currencies training event three months earlier approached me at a clergy gathering. "I have to tell you something exciting that happened since the workshop," she proclaimed.

"I was talking to the owner of a restaurant, which I frequently patronize, and remembered what you said about using our currency of relationship. I have known this owner for a while and had developed a trusting friendship with him. He knows I am a pastor. I realized that I had never asked him to come to church! So on that day, I decided to ask him. He said, 'I can't because my restaurant is open on Sunday and I have to be here.' I thought that was the end of that conversation. But then he said, 'What about doing church here in the restaurant?'"

So the pastor and the restaurant owner worked to create a worship service on Sunday, late in the afternoon. People started coming and most of them stayed afterward to have dinner. I congratulated her for creating an innovative ministry that was both missional and sustainable. She said, "My congregation had been trying to do missional work for years. I never thought it would so easy—just a shifting of the mind in how we think about our relationships and church."

> They went out and got into the boat, but that night they caught nothing. Just after daybreak, Jesus stood on the beach; but the disciples did not know that it was Jesus. Jesus said to them, "Children, you have no fish, have you?" They answered him, "No." He said to them, "Cast the net to the right side of the boat, and you will find some." So they cast it, and now they were not able to haul it in because there were so many fish. (John 21:3b–6)

40

Équi-Table: Going Missional in Quebec City

When participants in our Holy Currencies workshops practice what they have learned, they often get exciting results. The Rev. Darla Sloan was one of them. Here is her report:

> If going missional is about being with people where they are at and building relationships, then in Quebec City, a pub or a restaurant is where you have to be! People here today attend "happy hour" after work and weekend brunch more religiously then their ancestors attended Roman Catholic mass. I had often thought of taking the gospel into a local restaurant or pub as a way of inviting people to nourish their spirituality. But I was also aware that cash flow (or lack thereof) would prevent a number of people I knew from attending.
>
> Working through *Holy Currencies* with Eric got my wheels turning and I came up with the idea for Équi-Table.[27] The concept is simple. Gather a group of people in a local restaurant. People order what they want and pay what they can. If they can pay for their meal, great! If they can pay a little more, even better because it helps cover the cost of the meal of those who have a little less to share. I chose a restaurant that had sufficient parking and easy options for those travelling on public transit. I also wanted a restaurant with a play area so that kids could have a place to go if they got tired of listening to the grown-ups talk. Initially, I spoke with restaurant management to see if they would give us a "group rate" or something. No, they didn't do that sort of thing. Then I toyed with the idea of asking people to choose from a limited selection of menu items (to reduce the size of the final bill). In the end, I decided that I would just trust the Spirit and invite people to order whatever they wanted and pay what they could. I would pay the bill with my credit card and ask people to put their anonymous contributions in a small box placed in the center of the table. I told myself that if I needed to pay an astronomical amount to cover the shortfall at the end of the evening, I would know that I had to rethink things before trying again.

---

[27]Read about this ministry in French at https://celebrations5saisons.wordpress.com/equitable/.

So, on a Monday night in October 2012, a group of us gathered. We shared a meal and Kaleidoscope Bible study, followed by a celebration of the Lord's supper. (A woman in a clerical shirt draws a lot of attention in this town!) At the end of the evening I asked participants for feedback, and they responded that they liked having the opportunity to build relationships with new people and to do so while talking about their faith (because they said they didn't get much of an opportunity to do that in church!!). Participants liked hearing from people with different church backgrounds (or no church background).

The experiment worked! When I got home and opened the box in which everyone put what they could afford, there was just enough to cover the bill! And the same thing has happened again and again.

There have been some variations on the theme. We have decided to change restaurants in order to vary the menu, but also to have a room to ourselves. It does mean that we are less visible to the rest of the restaurant patrons. However, upon reflection, it was decided that the ultimate goal was to be able to build relationships around the table and that that is easier to do if we can hear each other well. In July of 2013, 11 adults and five children took Equi-Table outside (to two picnic tables near a playground in a park) and we feasted on loaves and fishes.

And since restaurants are not the only Quebec City attraction that are beyond the budgets of many, we have decided to take Equi-Table to the Museum of Fine Arts this fall. After we visit the museum, we'll gather around a table in the coffee shop and use "Mutual Invitation" to talk about the connection between art and our faith and spirituality.

And the wheel keeps on turning! Rather than being a block to participation, the currency of money has flowed and helped to create a ministry that is sustainable. We have made use of public spaces that are available to us. We have built relationships of trust where people feel free to speak the truth about their lives and their faith. And in taking time to nourish our bodies and our souls, we have nurtured our collective wellness. Praise God from whom all blessings flow!

The Rev. Darla Sloan

The rich and the poor have this in common:
the LORD is the maker of them all. (Proverbs 22:2)

41

The Beatitudes/Let Your Light So Shine

Blessed are the poor in spirit, for theirs is the kingdom of heaven.
Blessed are those who mourn, for they shall be comforted.
Blessed are the meek, for they shall inherit the earth.
Blessed are those who hunger and thirst for righteousness, for they
shall be satisfied.
Blessed are the merciful, for they shall obtain mercy.
Blessed are the pure in heart, for they shall see God.
Blessed are the peacemakers, for they shall be called children of God.
Blessed are those who are persecuted for righteousness' sake, for theirs
is the kingdom of heaven.
(Paraphrase, Matthew 5:3–10)

Christ is our guiding light.
Come, let us walk in the way of peace.

Let your light so shine.
Let your light so shine.
Let your light so shine before all people.
Let your light so shine.
Let your light so shine
So that all may see the glory of God.
(Paraphrase, Matthew 5:16)

The Beatitudes/Let Your Light So Shine

Principal Canon

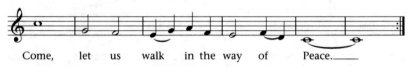

Christ is our guid - ing light:____

Come, let us walk in the way of Peace.____

Descant

Let your light so shine, let your light so shine, let your

light so shine be-fore all peo - ple.____ Let your light so shine, let your

light so shine, so that all may see the glo-ry of God.____

Accompaniment

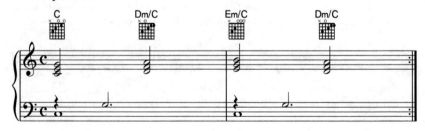

42

Reverse Stewardship

Many churches tend to think of the stewardship of money as a linear process. We ask people to give and we collect, and then we decide to give the money to worthy ministries. The holy currencies/cycle of blessings way of stewardship is a spiral and a dynamic process through which resources can be circulated through the neighborhood or community, and eventually return to sustain the churches' ministries as well as the wider community. Another idea to consider is something I call "reverse stewardship."

Instead of collecting money from people, the church gives each member some money—say, $20—and the church member is asked to invest that money back into the local neighborhood or community. The church also invites people to do a little research and make a list of businesses in their community that support the local economy. That is, these businesses utilize local resources and hire local people, and the owners live in the neighborhood and pay local property taxes. Church members are encouraged to spend their money supporting these local businesses.

Alternatively, church members can pool their money together in order to do things such as sponsoring a neighborhood sports team or starting a scholarship fund. This way, you are teaching church members—and this includes children—how money can be a currency that exchanges into blessings for the local community.

If your congregation does something like this every month, the church might become better known in the local community, and you will have increased your currency of relationship. A side benefit is that you are teaching your congregation to use the currency of money in an ethical manner to rejuvenate the local economy. When the local community is moving toward a healthier local economy as a result of "reverse stewardship" generated from your church, over time the money will come back to support the church through your expanded currencies of relationship, truth, and wellness.

> The point is this: the one who sows sparingly will also reap sparingly, and the one who sows bountifully will also reap bountifully... (2 Corinthians 9:6)

43

Reverse Musical Chairs

The children march around a circle of chairs as the music starts. When the music suddenly stops, they scramble to find a seat because there is always one less chair than the number of children marching. If you are not fast enough, you are "out." Eventually there will only be one winner. I hated musical chairs as a child because I was not the fastest kid, nor did I want to get into a fight with someone for a seat.

What did we learn from playing musical chairs when we were children? We might have learned something about scarcity (there is not enough for everyone) and something about competition (you have to be aggressive and quick in order to get your chair).

This is only one of many games, stories, and experiences through which our society has consciously and unconsciously instilled in us the spirituality of scarcity. I realize why it is so hard to teach holy currencies, which flows out of a spirituality of abundance—there is always enough if we share with others what we have. For those who have not done much reflection on living in abundance, this is a fundamental shift in the way they think about resources.

So, what can we do with musical chairs? I decided to design an alternative version, based on the spirituality of abundance. I call this game "reverse musical chairs."

> Start with three chairs and two players. The rest of the players sit in an outer circle of chairs facing in. The game begins with the two players introducing themselves by sharing something that they are good at (or another appropriate topic). As the music starts, the two players move around the three chairs and when the music stops, the two players sit down. The two players sitting next to the empty chair now invite the person closest to that chair from the outer circle to join the group. It is also the job of the two players to find out something that the new player is good at and then introduce him/her to the whole gathering. A new chair is added to the inner circle. Now we have three players and four chairs. The music starts again and when the music stops, the two players next to the empty chair invite another in. Another chair is added and so on. Eventually everyone will be in the inner circle.

A week after I posted the idea of "reverse musical chairs" on my blog, I received this letter from one of my associates, Jeannie Johnson:

Dear Eric,

I've just come home from leading an EfM (Education for Ministry) Training for Diocesan Coordinators at Sewanee. Your article about reverse musical chairs came just before I left, and it was the perfect forum in which to try it out.

The group of EfM Coordinators, from all over the U.S., had just returned from a brief trip, and I thought it would be a good transition back into the training. I did not introduce the exercise, except to say that, in classic EfM fashion, we are going to experience something and then reflect on it.

My co-trainer and I put three chairs in a row in the middle of the room (two facing one way and the one in the middle facing the opposite way). We chose two people to begin. Someone said, "Oh, this is musical chairs, but we have too many chairs."

We didn't say anything, and the music started. When it stopped, they grabbed chairs, and we asked them to invite someone to join them, and to find out something about that person that the rest of us didn't know, and then to introduce that information to the group. (If we had done this earlier in the training, I would have asked them to find out what the new person's gifts were—but we had done other exercises earlier that showed that information to the group.)

We kept adding chairs and people until everyone was in the chairs in the middle of the room.

I then asked them to reflect by saying, "What did you experience?" They talked about how much more fun it was to play when they knew they didn't have to fight for a chair. They also said how inclusive it was, and how they enjoyed finding out about the "new" person. And then they said how much this meant to them as new Diocesan Coordinators for EfM, because they realized that a big part of their job is to welcome people and include them into EfM!

Several people said they were going to use reverse musical chairs when they got home in their own Diocese and with their own EfM groups, and they all felt it was applicable in many different settings and situations.

I just thought you'd like to know!
Jeannie Johnson

If we played reverse musical chairs with our children and adults, the message that we would be teaching is that there is always room to include more, that it is our responsibility to invite others in, and that each person has something important to contribute. If these lessons are taught consistently to the next generations through more games and processes that are abundance-based, how would this impact the way we operate our economy? What would our healthcare system be like? What would our communities be like, if the majority of the people practiced this spirituality of abundance?

In my Father's house there are many dwelling places. If it were not so, would I have told you that I go to prepare a place for you? (John 14:2)

44

A Time to Play

One August morning in 1966, Charles Whitman, a seemingly normal, 25-year-old engineering student and former Marine sharpshooter, wheeled a trunk full of guns and ammunition onto the elevator of the tower overlooking the University of Texas campus. For three terrifying hours, he shot and killed 17 and wounded 41 university students and staff.[28] Why did a seemingly normal person—a former altar boy, the youngest American boy to become an Eagle Scout, someone with no criminal record—go berserk and commit the largest mass murder in U.S. history up to that time?

Dr. Stuart Brown, a psychiatrist at Baylor College of Medicine at the time—later to be founder of the National Institute for Play—was invited to join a team of researchers to solve this mystery. He discovered that Whitman grew up in an abusive household with a tyrannical father who, from the time he was born until age 18, forbade him to play. The committee concluded that the lifelong lack of play was a key factor in Whitman's homicidal actions. Without play, he was deprived of "opportunities to view life with optimism, test alternatives, or learn the social skills that, as part of spontaneous play, prepare individuals to cope with life stress."[29]

Brown continued his research with other violent individuals and concluded that "play can act as a powerful deterrent, even an antidote to prevent violence. Play is a powerful catalyst for positive socialization."[30]

According to the information at the website of the National Institute for Play, playing is good for your health and well-being. "It generates optimism, seeks out novelty, makes perseverance fun, leads to mastery, gives the immune system a bounce, fosters empathy and promotes a sense of belonging and community. Each of these play by-products are indices of personal health, and their shortage predicts impending health problems and personal fragility."

Playing is essential to build trusting, intimate relationships. "Play refreshes a long-term adult-adult relationship; some of the hallmarks of its refreshing, oxygenating action are: humor, the enjoyment of novelty, the capacity to share a lighthearted sense of the world's ironies, the enjoyment of mutual storytelling, the capacity to openly divulge imagination and

---

[28]The number killed and wounded varied from different reports. I got this information from the website of the National Institute for Play at http://www.nifplay.org/vision/early-study/.

[29]Most of the information about Dr. Brown and the National Institute for Play are from http://www.nifplay.org/vision/early-study/. Quotes in this chapter not otherwise identified are from this website.

[30]Ibid.

fantasies,... These playful communications and interactions, when nourished, produce a climate for easy connection and deepening, more rewarding relationship—true intimacy."

Playing is also a catalyst for learning for any age. "When students have fun at learning, they continue to pursue it for its own sake. It is how nature assured us how to learn about the world and our places in it."

> "But to what will I compare this generation? It is like children sitting
> in the marketplaces and calling to one another,
>> 'We played the flute for you, and you did not dance;
>>> we wailed, and you did not mourn.'"(Matthew 11:16–17)

Jesus compared the generation of people around him to children who did not want to or know how to play. He continued, " For John came neither eating nor drinking, and they say, 'He has a demon'; the Son of Man came eating and drinking, and they say, 'Look, a glutton and a drunkard, a friend of tax collectors and sinners!'" (Matthew 11:18–19). In other words, Jesus was saying that they didn't have a sense of humor. They only made judgment and were not able to play and explore. He was referring to the people who would eventually put him to death.

I am not saying that if we don't play, we will end up becoming mass murderers. But I can say that if we overlook the role of play in our lives, it will probably be bad for our relationships and well-being. Investing your currencies of time and place in play will exchange them into deeper relationships, greater wellness, and enhanced gracious leadership.

The Kaleidoscope Institute uses many play elements in our training. We use role-play and scripted play, inviting participants to imagine and pretend. We use movement such as body sculptures to engage participants in discovering relationships and community organization. We use body movement for Bible study to help participants embody the text. We take notecards, sticky notes, photos, and art supplies and invite participants to write on them, play with them, arrange them, and make new objects out of them.

Stuart Brown, in his book *Play,* wrote, "Of all animal species, humans are the biggest players of all. We are built to play and built through play. When we play, we are engaged in the purest expression of our humanity, the truest expression of our individuality. Is it any wonder that often the times we feel most alive, those that make up our best memories, are moments of play?"[31]

In what ways can you incorporate play into your personal life and your family? How can play be part of your gracious leadership skill set in your work and ministry? How do you enable people in your community to invest time and place in taking a Sabbath in which they can play?

---

[31]Stuart Brown with Christopher Vaughan, *Play* (New York: Penguin Group, 2009), 5.

45

Active Leisure

At the end of 2013, I took a three-month sabbatical. I decided to take the first week of my sabbatical and do nothing. As expected, I struggled with doing nothing—but not because I am a workaholic, as my partner would call me. I struggled with my mind continuing to be active—wanting to read books that were work-related, sitting down at the piano and ending up writing a song, listening to a friend's concerns and feeling like I was working as pastoral counselor; I couldn't let go of the need to work!

"The popular assumption is that no skills are involved in enjoying free time, and that anybody can do it," Mihaly Csikszentmihalyi wrote in *Finding Flow*, "yet evidence suggests the opposite: free time is more difficult to enjoy than work. Having leisure at one's disposal does not improve the quality of life unless one knows how to use it effectively, and it is by no means something one learns automatically."[32]

Reading *Finding Flow* stopped me from beating myself up for not knowing how to do nothing. Csikszentmihalyi makes the distinction between passive and active leisure time. Passive leisure engages in activities that do not require skills or much concentration, such as watching TV, watching a movie, or reading an unchallenging book. While I appreciate the fact that people need time to relax and unwind, I believe the exclusive use of passive leisure for our free time can negatively impact our lives. For example, passive leisure activities such as watching TV can stop the flow of relationship. Clay Shirky, in *Cognitive Surplus*, says that "underinvesting in relational activities means spending less time with friends and family, precisely because watching a lot of TV leads us to shift more energy to material satisfaction and less to social satisfaction."[33]

Csikszentmihalyi explains that active leisure requires one to "devote as much ingenuity and attention to it as one would to one's job... In the past leisure was justified because it gave people an opportunity to experiment and to develop skills. In fact, before science and the arts became professionalized, a great deal of scientific research, poetry, painting, and musical composition was carried out in a person's free time... Nowadays only experts are supposed to be interested in such issues;... But amateurs—those who do something because they love to do it—add enjoyment and interest to their own life and to everybody else's."[34]

---

[32]Mihaly Csikszentmihalyi, *Finding Flow* (New York: Basics Book, 1997), 65.
[33]Clay Shirky, *Cognitive Surplus* (London: Penguin Book, 2010), 8.
[34]Csikszentmihalyi, *Finding Flow*, 75.

Wellness is not achieved by doing mindless things. Wellness is achieved by freeing our minds and bodies to explore, to experiment, to create, and to play. Sabbath is active leisure time. It is a time to pay attention to my relationship with myself, with others, with the environment, and with God. During Sabbath, we notice the truth, the reality about our relationships and our community. We want to learn more about how to achieve understanding of self, others, and God. During Sabbath, we find creative means of exchanging this knowledge, exploring new ways to improve our lives.

For the rest of my sabbatical, I read books, even though they seemed to be work-related; I wrote poetry and songs, which I used for my workshops in the following years; I visited ministries I found interesting. I sat and listened to stories of friends and strangers. And I also spent time watching TV, going to movies, and reading mindless detective novels. The key is that I did not feel guilty, nor did I struggle with actively thinking and paying attention during my sabbatical.

Most middle-upper-class people in the U.S. spent one-third of their day sleeping, one-third working or going to school, and one-third enjoying free time. What if we found a way to empower people to use their surplus free time as active leisure time? Imagine what this currency of time could be exchanged for—maybe new music, poetry, art, dance, inventions, relationships, truth, and, of course, wellness.

46

Come and I Will Give You Rest

For too long I've sung the freedom songs
For too long I've marched to right the wrongs
Nothing ever really changed
Evil's pattern simply rearranged
And I'm tired; I'm falling
All my hopes are stalling
Then I hear a gentle voice calling:
Come, come to me, all of you who are weary
Come, as you are, all of you who are heavy laden
Come and I will give you rest
Come
For too long I've run the righteous race
Could this world be running out of grace?
I'm afraid we'll lose our souls
In this world of merciless controls
And I'm tired; I'm falling
All my dreams are crawling
Then I hear a gentle voice calling
Come, come to me, all of you who are weary
Come, as you are, all of you who are heavy laden
Come and I will give you rest
Come
Take my yoke upon you and learn from me
My yoke is easy
My breath is breezy
Breathe my spirit in you; discern from me
I'm not judgmental
My heart is gentle
With the common passion that we share
We will ease the burden that you bear
Come with your friends, with your foes, and your quarrels
Come with your rage, with wounds and your battered morals
Come with your fear, with your loss, and your sorrow
Come with your frail, faded hope of a just tomorrow
Come with your cold, burnt-out souls and your yearnings
Come, I'll ignite flames of hope and we'll keep them burning
Come and I will give you rest
Come

Come and I Will Give You Rest

Come and I____will give__you rest.__ So come._____

2. Come._____ Take my yoke up-on you and learn from me._____ My yoke is eas-y_____ My breath is bree- zy._____ Breathe my spir - it in you, dis - cern from me._____ I'm not judg men- tal;_____ my heart is gen- tle.__ With the com-mon pas-sion that we share,___ we will ease the bur - den that you bear._____

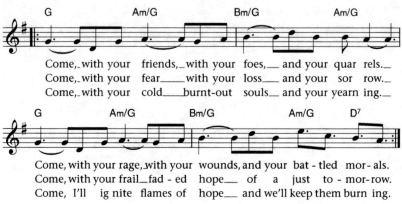

Come,_with your friends,_with your foes,_ and your quar rels._
Come,_with your fear____with your loss__ and your sor row._
Come,_with your cold____burnt-out souls__ and your yearn ing._

Come, with your rage,_with your wounds, and your bat - tled mor- als.
Come, with your frail_fad - ed hope__ of a just to - mor-row.
Come, I'll ig nite flames of hope__ and we'll keep them burn ing.

3

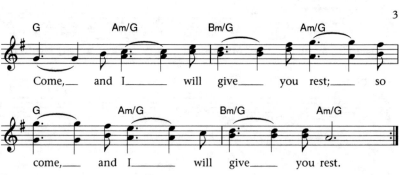

Come,__ and I_____ will give____ you rest;____ so

come,__ and I_____ will give____ you rest.

47

Pledge Card for Currency of Time

Time, talent, and treasure are the trinity of resources that most stewardship campaigns talk about. In these approaches, we are asking members of the church to contribute their time, talent, and treasure for ministries facilitated by the church. For a holy currencies/cycle of blessings stewardship approach, we expand the stewardship campaign to include external time, talent, and treasure. Here is a holy currency pledge card for time.

There are three kinds of time commitments. First, church members are asked to make the standard commitment of time for existing and new ministries of the church. Second, we invite members to commit to offering time to ministries outside the church that may or may not be ministries created and facilitated by the church. Why is this important? When we spend time supporting the ministries that foster wellness in our neighborhood, we are creating a more sustainable community together. A sustainable community will, in turn, support the church that gives time to help create a sustainable community. Finally, this pledge card prompts church members to invite people outside the church to volunteer time to support worthy ministries. For example, a church that is near a college can invite students to volunteer at the church's food ministry. A church can do many exciting and relevant ministries if the leadership can find ways to harvest the free-time surplus from the people in the neighborhood.

Pledge Card for Currency of Time

- I commit _____ hours per week for _____ (name of existing or new ministry in the church).
- I commit _____ hours per week for _____ (name of existing or new ministry in the community/neighborhood).
- I commit to invite _____ persons from the neighborhood/ community to volunteer _____ hours for _____ (name of existing or new ministry).

My name: _____ My accountable person: _____

_____   _____
    signature   signature

Date: _____

48

Psalm 23

Psalm 23 is one the best-known and best-loved texts in the Bible. It has been used in many funeral and memorial services. Composers have set this text to music. It begins:

The Lord is my shepherd, I shall not want.

The image of God as a shepherd might have been a common idea when the psalm was composed. Perhaps many who sang this psalm were shepherds themselves or they knew a real shepherd in their daily life. But today, how many of us know a real shepherd? The image of God as the shepherd can be quite foreign for us today. As I read the psalm and try to capture the relationship between God and her people, I realize that this relationship is quite simple.

He makes me lie down in green pastures and leads me beside still waters.

A shepherd knows where the green pastures and sources of water are (sustenance for the sheep) and leads the sheep to these sources.

Though I walk through the valley of the shadow of death,
I shall fear no evil; for you are with me . . .

A shepherd provides a safe environment so that the sheep do not live in fear of scarcity but in the assurance of abundance.

...my cup is running over.

In other words, the shepherd is a gracious leader who lives the cycle of blessings.

A gracious leader knows the needs of people in the community. A gracious leader knows from where the resources for wellness flow. A gracious leader enables the people to connect with, utilize, and benefit from these sources. A gracious leader protects the people in the community from harm, assuring them that an abundance of resources can feed everyone spiritually, physically, socially, and economically.

Surely [your] goodness and mercy shall follow me
all the days of my life . . .

49

Like a Mother Eagle

If we live the cycle of blessings, we need to make our currencies "holy" by spending them according to God's pattern and will. Our concept of God becomes crucial in the way we relate to God and other human beings. Walter Wink, a biblical scholar and author, in a workshop titled "Transforming Bible Study" that I attended many years ago, said, "Preachers and teachers in faith community have a great responsibility. We are in the business of shaping people's God image." Our God image can empower us to do great things. Our God image can also cause us to do horrible things to people and to the environment. If I believe in an exclusive male-imaged God, this would impact the way I treat women, because I do not imagine them as part of the Divine. If my image of God is exclusively a vengeful lord who punishes his enemies, I would probably act in similar ways toward my own enemies.

Christians have their favorite God images, such as father, lord, shepherd, creator, sustainer, and redeemer. But, in the Bible, there are many images of God that can empower us to look beyond the boundaries of prescribed images. These images of God can help us to be more inclusive of others, fostering wellness and creating sustainable community. I find this particular text from Deuteronomy to be both challenging and comforting:

As an eagle stirs up its nest,
      and hovers over its young;
as it spreads its wings, takes them up,
      and bears them aloft on its pinions,
the Lord alone guided him;
      no foreign god was with him.
[She] set him atop the heights of the land,
      and fed him with produce of the field;
[She] nursed him with honey from the crags,
      with oil from flinty rock;
curds from the herd, and milk from the flock,
      with fat of lambs and rams;
Bashan bulls and goats,
      together with the choicest wheat—
      you drank fine wine from the blood of grapes.
(Deuteronomy 32:11–14)

This text is challenging because I am asked to learn to fly and I am afraid of heights; comforting because God is there supporting me like a mother eagle. Living the cycle of blessings is like learning to fly for the first time: we need all the help we can get. I love this God image so much that I put these verses (with some modification, especially the pronunciation) to music.

Like a Mother Eagle

C

ea - gle,_____ like a moth-er
ea - gle,_____ like a moth-er

D

ea - gle._____
ea - gle._____

Accompaniment

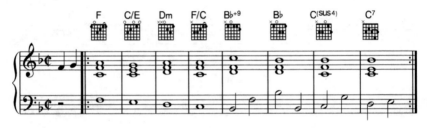

F   C/E   Dm   F/C   Bb+9   Bb   C(SUS4)   C7

50

Waste Water into Wine

I was leading a weeklong training workshop in an area of California surrounded by vineyards. Many members of the group I was training also enjoyed a glass of wine each evening to unwind. For several years now, California has been experiencing a severe drought, and because of that, I pay attention to how water is used and recycled everywhere I go. In my research, I had discovered that many California wineries were using recycled wastewater for irrigation. While I was sipping my wine, I had this uneasy feeling that this tasty and aromatic liquid might at one time have been wastewater! I knew the wastewater had been treated. But still, the idea of drinking wastewater was a little disconcerting.

Then I took a deep breath and enjoyed the "bouquet" of my wine, and gave thanks to the amazing plants that produce grapes. The plant functions as a recycling device; it not only filters the water being drawn up through its vine, it transforms that water into sweet juice in grapes, which we reap and transform into wine. A person who lives the cycle of blessings and practices the exchanges of holy currencies learns from the plants and trees on this earth. The lessons we learn from this amazing part of God's creation will help us recycle and transform our waste into resources in all that we do. The lessons we learn will help us know how to sustain our communities and the earth.

What lessons have you learned from God's creation about missional and sustainable ministries?

When you send forth your spirit, they are created;
and you renew the face of the ground. (Psalm 104:30)

51

Sustaining Tree

I was honored to be part of Brandon and Bharti's wedding, which took place in Santa Monica under a giant fig tree that is more than 100 years old. When it was time for me to offer my remarks, I couldn't help but be inspired by this magnificent tree. Here is a summary of what I said:

There are many ways to appreciate a tree. We can admire its strength, height, and width, and how it provides shade and shelter for us. We can marvel at the extension of its roots above the ground. We can see that there were branches that have been broken off, and yet the tree continues to grow with new branches next to it. We can appreciate the many fruit it bears.

But these are only the external things that we can see of a tree. What makes up a tree that is over 100 years old involves many other things. There is the earth through which the roots of the tree can hold the tree up above. The earth works with water and feeds the tree through its root system. Then there is the air and the sun interacting with the leaves through the photosynthesis process, giving us fresh air to breath. A tree is not just a tree. It has to interact and be supported by all of these other elements. When a tree is established and strong, it can withstand many things and still stay strong. If we have a draught, for example, this tree will survive because its roots reach very deep into the ground to find water down there. If there is a big storm and many of its branches are broken off, it will survive and sprout new branches. This tree is sustainable because of all the elements surrounding it, making it strong.

There are many ways to appreciate a wedding. We can admire the beautiful couple and their friends in the wedding party. We can see the beautiful flowers and decorations, wonderful food and the delicious wedding cake. But what makes a strong marriage involves not just the love between two persons getting married. It involves their families and their friends. They are the ones who are like the earth, the water, the air, and the sun that will nurture the couple's relationship, allowing their love for each other to grow deep roots, keeping their marriage strong.

And when marriage needs to weather a storm—perhaps an emotional one or a physical one—the marriage will stay sustainable because of friends and family surrounding the couple.

Responding to God's call to create sustainable communities requires us to make a commitment to live the cycle of blessings. In order to sustain this commitment, we need all the currencies flowing, especially a strong relationship network. How are your family and friendship networks involved in supporting this movement? Who will provide the wellness currencies? Who will challenge you to face the truth? Who will coach you with gracious leadership?

52

Healing Leaves

> Then the angel showed me the river of the water of life, bright as crystal, flowing...through the middle of the street of the city. On either side of the river is the tree of life with its twelve kinds of fruit, producing its fruit each month; and the leaves of the tree are for the healing of the nations. (Revelations 22:1–2)

When we look at a beautiful scene, such as the one described above, in a painting, a photo, a video, or in reality, we tend to pay attention to the bright and sparkly parts that stand out from the rest of the scene, such as the water that is bright as crystal, and the fruit or flowers that the tree produces. Sometimes, we overlook the most essential part of the picture—the leaves on the trees. Yes, the flowing water of life sparkling in the sun is important. So is the fruit that a tree produces to give us food. But the leaves do most or all of the work—converting the energy of the sun, the water source, and things we consider waste—such as carbon dioxide—into oxygen and food. This is why in the vision from the book of Revelation, "the leaves of the tree are for the healing of the nations."

The earth and the nations are not well because we don't have enough people and communities who can act like leaves—transforming wastes into resources that will regenerate and rejuvenate human communities and the earth. How can the earth be healed when we throw away so many material things every day, with little thoughts of recycling them? How can our nations be healed when we throw away so many people who we consider useless—evidenced by the overcrowding of prisons in the U.S., children dying of hunger around the world, or innocent people dying in wars? Yes, the sun is always present and the water of life is flowing, and we know that there is enough for everyone and every nation on this earth. However, without the transforming power of the leaves, there is no healing.

Gracious leaders who live the cycle of blessings act like leaves. We see and acknowledge the abundance all around us, but we also consciously take part in the circulation of resources, transforming waste and taking the throwaways, and recirculating them back into cyclical flow.

53

Giant Corn Fields and Community Gardens

Once, I took a cross-country ride on Amtrak from Los Angeles to Chicago, then from Chicago to New York City. I had great fun posting photos on Facebook along the way. By the time I arrived in New York, more than 100 of my friends were following me on this visual journey.

One thing that stayed with me from my trip was the vastness of the farms in the middle of the country. I have always been a city person—I grew up in Hong Kong and New York City. Twenty years ago, I would have looked at these huge farms and had nothing but praiseworthy thoughts: What great amount of food these farms produce! What wonderful technologies are used to make these farms work!

But now I have conflicting thoughts about these big farms: What have been the impacts of these farms on the environment? How are the workers treated? What happens to the smaller farms and farmers?

These conflicting thoughts were still swimming in my head when I arrived at Westminster Presbyterian Church in Trenton, New Jersey, to preach at the congregation's 115th anniversary service. Before worship began, I was given a tour of the facility. The pastor, Rev. Karen Hernandez-Granzen, proudly showed me a small raised-bed community garden by the side of the church building. Later in the service, a multi-media presentation about Bethany House of Hospitality included mention of a more expanded community garden.

The contrast between community gardens in the city and huge farms in the country helped me realize what was bothering me. A community garden includes a diversity of plants, such as tomatoes, peppers, herbs, squash, and corn. The garden brings people together. As they work with the earth, experience the miracle of growing food, and celebrate the harvest, they connect with each other and with the earth.

Although a large farm produces an enormous amount of food efficiently, and I am grateful for the technologies involved, it also creates a distance between everyday people and the earth. What percentage of the citizens of the United States really know where the corn-on-the-cob they eat on Labor Day comes from, or how it was grown?

I am not against big farms. A sustainable community networks globally and connects locally. Through the big farms, we produce food to feed people globally; at least, this is my hope. (In fact, I know that we produce enough food in the U.S. to feed everyone in the world; and, yet, people around the world go to bed hungry—a problem that needs to be solved by maximizing our global network.) However, a sustainable community needs also to feed people locally with locally grown produce. In doing so, we not only feed people physically, we are also feeding people spiritually and socially, building up local relationship networks that, in the long run, are at the heart of a sustainable community.

54

Cycle of Blessings

I was in New York City visiting family one winter day in 2014. The snow started falling mid-morning and continued nonstop for at least 10 hours, covering the concrete and steel landscape with 13 inches of snow. During the day, I watched as the people in the city slowed down. Even the businesses in Chinatown, which seemed always to be open, were closing early and sending their workers home.

We can think of these snowstorms as inconveniences to our daily lives. We can also come to understand them as necessary for the sustainability of life on earth. In fact, the state of New York needed that many inches of precipitation to maintain a normal water supply level that year. And being slowed down and getting home early could be a welcome change—a little unexpected Sabbath-wellness time. In spite of humanity's role in contributing to global climate change, nature is still providing us with what we need, though perhaps in extreme ways. Are we willing to do our part in balancing the cycle of blessings on this wonderful, challenging earth we all share?

As rain and snow fall from the sky,
They won't return until
They have cleansed and watered the earth.
Flowing through plants;
Making them grow;
Plenteous food for all to eat,
Bearing new seeds for us to sow
Making the cycle of blessings complete.
So the Word of God comes from on high,
It won't return until
Love is circling throughout the earth.
Filling our hearts;
Making us whole;
Spiritual feast for all to eat,
Bounteous grace to seed our souls
Making the cycle of blessings complete
As rain and snow fall from the sky,
They won't return until
They have cleansed and watered the earth.
So the Word of God comes from on high,
It won't return until
Love is circling through out the earth.
(Inspired by Isaiah 55:10–11)

Cycle of Blessings

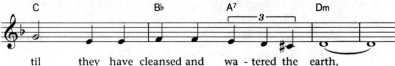

As the rain and snow   fall   from the sky;   they won't re-turn un -
So the Word of God   comes from on high;   it   won't re-turn un -

til   they have cleansed and   wa - tered the   earth,
til   Love   is   cir - cling through-out the   earth,

Flow-ing through plants;   mak-ing them grow;   plen te-ous food for
Fill - ing   our   hearts,   mak-ing us whole;   spi - ri-tual feast for

all   to   eat.   Bear-ing new seeds for   us   to   sow,
all   to   eat.   Boun-te - ous grace to   seed   our souls,

mak-ing the cy-cle of bless-ings com   -   plete._____   So the
mak-ing the cy-cle of bless-ings com   -   plete._____   As the

rain and snow fall   from the sky; they won't re-turn un - til they have
Word of God comes from on high; it   won't re-turn un - til love is

cleansed and   wa - tered the   earth.___   So the
cir - cling through-out the_____   earth.___

55

Pledge Card for Currency of Wellness

We've once again come to the part of the book in which I ask you to make a pledge involving one of the currencies. This time, it is the currency of wellness. In working through the cycle of blessings, we often begin by naming the truth of the unwellness in our lives and communities. Achieving wellness becomes the mission of our ministries. The yearning to foster wellness drives the way we invest our other currencies.

With this pledge card, we are doing a slightly different take on wellness. First, we invite church members to consciously commit to taking good care of themselves physically, socially, and spiritually. "Sabbatical activity" refers to setting aside time and place to pay attention to our wellness—physical exercise; spending time with loved ones, friends, and strangers; reading, resting, playing, praying, and other life-giving activities. Second, we invite church members to commit to sabbatical activities that foster wellness within the church community. These may include creating a church community retreat; having meaningful conversations about current concerns; eating together; hiking, bicycling, and exercising as a group; family game day; prayer groups; and bible study groups; Third, we invite church members to create Sabbath for the people living in the church's neighborhood. People, whether they belong to a faith community or not, are extremely busy these days. Most people have lost a sense of the rhythm and balance between work, rest, and play. Church members can intentionally create neighborhood events to help the community regain this balance for wellness. Neighborhood sabbatical activities can include a block party, health fair, community garden, farmer's market, or a day of family fun with games and conversation. Finally, we invite church members to consider participating in activities that foster wellness for the earth—planting a tree, cleaning up the environment, creating green space in the neighborhood, encouraging others to recycle, and using renewable energy.

Take some time to make a commitment for any or all of the sabbatical activities. Find an Accountable Person, tell him or her about your commitment, and have him or her witness and sign the card. Submit it to your church leaders. If they don't know what this card is, have a great conversation explaining currency of wellness with them.

Pledge Card for Currency of Wellness

- I commit to take part in _____ (name sabbatical activity) for my own physical, social, and spiritual wellness.
- I commit to take part in _____ (name sabbatical activity) in order to increase the social, physical, and spiritual wellness of my family, friends, and people in my church community.
- I commit to take part in _____ (name sabbatical activity) in order to increase the social, physical, and spiritual wellness of the people living in my neighborhood.
- I commit to take part in _____ (name sabbatical activity) in order to enhance the ecological wellness of my neighborhood, my city/town, and my country.

My name:_____ My accountable person: _____

_____   _____
    signature   signature

Date: _____

56

When I Pour Out My Spirit

June 4, 2014, marked the 25th anniversary of the Tiananmen Square massacre in China, which left an unknown number of Chinese pro-democracy protesters dead. This event silenced a hopeful democratic movement that inspired the world, but threatened the Chinese government leaders who ordered the attacks on their own people. As the anniversary date approached, the Chinese government began making arrests to preempt any potential protests to commemorate this event. If violence and evocation of fear worked the first time, why wouldn't it work again?

In 25 years, China has become the one of the largest economies in the world, and yet, fear still reigns. China may have become a great nation in the eyes of many, but will it be sustainable in the long run if it continues to rely on fear to silence the voices of the powerless in order to hold the nation together?

> Your sons and daughters shall prophesy,
>> your old shall dream dreams,
>> and your young shall see visions.
> Even on my servants, both men and women, I will pour out my Spirit in those days. (Joel 2:28–29, paraphrased) [35]

Almost 2,000 years ago during Pentecost, a Jewish festival celebrated 50 days after Passover, a small group of Jews who followed a teacher named Jesus claimed that this prophecy was fulfilled. A few days prior to Pentecost, the risen Jesus had bidden farewell to his followers and ascended to heaven, leaving them without a leader and feeling powerless. Certainly no one would expect them to be spokespersons for God. But on that Pentecost Day, they prophesied. Perhaps the real miracle was that the crowd who had come for the Pentecost feast was there when they did. The crowd members heard this small group of people speaking, in the native tongues of the hearers, about God's deeds of power. Many became believers as a result.

We are living in a world dominated by the voices of the powerful and rich. They can manipulate political systems to make us believe that we are indeed powerless. Their influential voices are moving us away from a sustainable future for all. We need a Pentecost now. Not only in China; we need a Pentecost all around the world, through which we can hear the dreams, visions, and prophecies of the powerless.

---

[35] I have made a music video with these words. You can view it at http://www.youtube.com/watch?v=eutOKzgLXcE.

With the Internet, the World Wide Web, and smartphones, we are more able to hear the prophetic voices of the powerless. YouTube, for example, offers everyone who has a computer or smartphone with a camera, free of charge, the ability to broadcast his or her voice and image to millions. Social media allows people to network globally with each other, bypassing the systems controlled by the rich and powerful in our societies.

Gracious leaders, who live the cycle of blessing, need to listen to the voices of the powerless. We need to help them network with others, locally and globally, to find their voice together. We can do that by providing access to technologies that empower and amplify their voices. The fact is, there are more powerless people in the world than there are powerful ones. There are more poor people than rich. If we can network and hear each other, support each other, and let our voices be amplified and circulated through our connections, then there is hope for a Pentecost in which the powerful would finally listen. When the dreams, visions, and prophecies of the poor and powerless are listened to, perhaps there is hope for a sustainable future in which everyone is affirmed, not just a powerful few.

Where are the prophets for our world today? The prophetic voices of our time have to come from the powerless ones in our midst. They will tell us where resources are not flowing and recirculating. They will tell us where in our network are the places of unsustainability, because they are the ones who are suffering. But even if they are prophesying, are we listening?

When I Pour Out My Spirit

Gather your community and watch the YouTube video: *When I Pour Out My Spirit.*

1. Invite the people who are gathered to reflect on the question: Who are the powerless ones in your family, community, neighborhood, town, or city, nation, and the world?
2. Ask them to share these reflections.
3. Invite them to further reflect on the question: In what ways can we follow the Spirit of Pentecost and listen to the powerless to hear their visions, dreams, and prophecies?

When I Pour Out My Spirit

After singing Theme I a few times, add the other themes progressively.

When I pour out my spir-it on all hu - man - kind:

Theme II

Your sons and daught-ers shall pro-phe - sy.

Theme III

Your old shall dream dreams.

Theme IV

Your young shall see vis - ions.

Theme V

When I pour out my spir - it on

all hu - - man - - kind.

57

Morning—April 14, 2015

I woke up this morning with holy currencies on my mind. What will the currency exchanges be today? I am two weeks away from having to finish the manuscript for this book. I plan on spending at least three solids hours this morning writing, and then at least two hours in the afternoon editing what I have written. I know when I am writing, I tunnel and ignore the things and people around me; so, taking an hour for lunch to be fully present with my loved one will be a challenge, but I can and will do it to maintain my currency of relationship and wellness. Dinner with my loved one is not negotiable, and it is good to have it as the start of my Sabbath time. We are also meeting a good friend mid-afternoon for tea. Oh, and I must not forget to set aside some physical wellness time—the currency I often neglect. So going to the gym late in the afternoon is a must. I also remember that my gym is hosting a social at 5 p.m. I should stay a while after my workout to meet some folks in my neighborhood.

So there it is, my day of currency exchanges. I exchange my currency of time and place today to create a document that hopefully will exchange into gracious leadership for future readers; I am most excited about this exchange. The published book will exchange into income for my publisher and royalties for me a year from now—the currency of money. Going to the gym will increase personal physical wellness currency, and staying for the reception will increase my currency of external relationship. Tea with a friend will strengthen my internal relationship currency. Being fully present at lunch and dinner with my loved one will maintain my currency of social and physical wellness.

These are the choices I make today. As I make these choices, I try to move these exchanges toward what is holy—that which is in the pattern of God's will—as best I can.

What are your holy currency exchanges today? How are you flowing your currencies toward the holy?

[A]s he who called you is holy, be holy yourselves in all your conduct; for it is written, "You shall be holy, for I am holy." (1 Peter 1:15–16)

58

The Holy Currency Mind

Since *Holy Currencies* was published in 2013, many readers have embraced the cycle of blessings and have begun to practice and teach these ideas to the people in their ministries. Do an Internet search on "holy currencies" and you will find sermons, study guides, discussion groups, diagrams, articles, and videos about this dynamic model of sustainable and missional ministry. Here is the first part of a sermon given by the Rev. Heather Leslie Hammer of Lynnewood United Methodist Church on August 4, 2013, which demonstrates her adoption of a holy currency mind-set—seeing everything in terms of holy currency exchanges:

> We are in the process of remodeling our kitchen. Some of you know what that is like. Last Tuesday we had to have everything out of the kitchen—canned goods, baking goods, pots, pans, glassware, dishes, vases, candles, cookbooks, and then there's what our family calls the miscellaneous drawer! Oh, my goodness! We have a corner cupboard that's hard to get to; you have to get down on your hands and knees and reach in to pull out the things that have worked their way into that far back corner over the 29 years we have lived in the house. And what surprises we found back there! Things we had completely forgotten we had. Wedding gifts, antique hand-me-downs from our parents, and things we honestly didn't remember ever having. In one of my more organized moments, I had made a list of all the things that were back in there. But I had long since forgotten all about the list, until I pulled it out this week. What good were those things doing, stored out of the way? Though at one point they were deemed to have been of value, now we had to admit that those "treasures" certainly were not ever being used. And if we hadn't missed those things in 29 years, would we ever even use them?
>
> So off they went to the thrift store. Tri-Valley Haven has a new thrift store in Livermore on Railroad Avenue. It used to be run by Buenas Vidas Youth Ranch, which is no more. I hope Lynnewood will support this new thrift store perhaps by helping to refurbish it along with our Circuit.[36] The building needs a lot of repair. I've been in this store many times. It is a gathering place of people looking for

---

[36] "Circuit" refers to a group of clergy (8–12) in the same area coming together regularly to support each other and collaborate in ministries.

bargains and for food. Someone had donated a big box of bananas on Monday when I was there dropping off my box of "treasures." While I looked around, a man came in and took some of the free bananas, maybe eight. It made me glad to think that his family would be having bananas for dinner and for breakfast. While I was there I spotted a handmade chalice. It made me wonder who had made it, and who had donated it; and then I thought, we could use another chalice here at church for communion. I bought it for $2. That $2 will be supper for a woman and her child at TriValley Haven, a shelter for families suffering from domestic violence. And then I thought about the people working at the thrift store. This place is giving women jobs. It's giving children inexpensive clothes to wear to school. It's giving families who move to this area pots and pans to set up kitchens. Maybe someone will even put to use that yellow metal fondue pot I brought in.

Thrift stores are places of recycling. Treasures aren't much good stored in corner cabinets. They are meant to be shared and used. In fact, a real treasure is one that converts into relationship and wellness and grace and truth.

Have you adopted a holy currencies mindset? How are you experiencing people, places, and things if you have done so? What changes will you make in the way you use your resources?

59

What Is This Thing Called Holy Currencies?

Many participants in the Holy Currencies workshops and presentations that I have given have returned home and taken on the challenge of explaining these dynamic and complex concepts to the people within their churches and ministries. Some have told me that it was not easy. My response is always: "Put it in context." The cycle of blessings becomes tangible when the currencies are connected with what people are already doing. From there, we can then talk about how to "flow" them or exchange them for blessings for others and the community. The second part of the Rev. Heather Leslie Hammer's sermon on August 4, 2013, attempted to do just that, but wisely put the holy currencies model in the context of what was already happening in Lynnewood United Methodist Church:

> At Annual Conference this year a man named Eric Law presented the ideas from his book, Holy Currencies. Eric Law is an Episcopal priest and leadership trainer. He talked about six currencies that most churches have. You can think of them as assets, or blessings. They convert into other assets or blessings when we use them to benefit, not ourselves, but others.
>
> The first currency is the currency of time and place. Think about our currency of time and place here at Lynnewood. We have the time that volunteers and staff offer to one another and to the community. An example would be our Stephen Ministers who give one-on-one time to be with people in crisis or in difficult transitions. Their time converts into healing and wellness. Our currency of place is the resource we have in our physical facility. Our facility has been a real asset, especially in that it is in use Monday through Friday by Quarry Lane Preschool. Our space is being converted to education and wellness, as well as into rental income for the church. We might think of how we could use our new youth room during the week. We might also think about how our facility could be an even better asset, if it were more welcoming to the public. (How many people do you know who do not know that our church is located here on Black Avenue?) The best use of our currencies is to share them with people who need them more than we do. An example of this kind of sharing is the way we encourage Alcoholics Anonymous groups

to use our classrooms on weeknights. We are exchanging time and place for other blessings.

The next currency is the currency of gracious leadership. This asset is the kind of leadership that fosters grace—it's not an authoritarian kind of leadership. It's the kind of leadership we have in the church when people are encouraged to work together, when new people's ideas are welcome, when people cooperate together to help people less fortunate than they are. This kind of currency translates into better relationships. Gracious leadership means using power and expertise, not for our own benefit, but instead to benefit the common good.

The currency of relationship is the blessing we have here in our church when we realize that nothing is more important than getting together and fostering God's love. Everything we do should lead to better relationships with God and with our neighbors. Hopefully our relationships will grow beyond our walls.

Building relationships leads to knowing the truth. When people trust each other, they will speak from their hearts. So, one currency leads to another. When we care about relationships with people who are different from us, we learn new truths. (If you know a Muslim family, you may know that they are now celebrating Ramadan, fasting each day.) We can understand from a new point of view. At our retreat in the fall, we will learn new ways to be sensitive to different cultures. Hopefully, this will lead to accepting new truths.

Many of these currencies, when converted, lead to wellness. The wellness must be inclusive. If my neighbor is not well, how can I be well? Finally, the currency of wellness brings about the currency of money. When a church is well and vital, people want to give. Wellness means all people have enough, and so those with much are asked to share with those with little. The currency of money returns us to where we started. Money is an asset that buys us staff time and facility space. The cycle of blessing begins again and flows like running water or, we could say, like living water.

How would you explain holy currencies and cycle of blessings to the people in your church or ministry? How would you use the context of your church and community to make these concepts real and accessible?

60

Embodying the Cycle of Blessings

Explaining holy currencies verbally and intellectually can only get you so far. Like most training workshops that I provide, the people need to be invited to act out—embody—the cycle of blessings by doing something concrete. The third part of the Rev. Heather Leslie Hammer's sermon initiated and mobilized the cycle of blessings by inviting her congregation, Lynnewood United Methodist, to do something concrete that would demonstrate the way of holy currencies.

To start this cycle today, I am making an investment. I have taken out of Jim's and my personal bank account $200, which I want to give to you today, a dollar per person, with the trust that you will use this dollar to continue the cycle of blessings. So, while our ushers are handing out one dollar bill to each person, I invite you to think with me what you can do with a dollar. Now you might say, you can't buy much with a dollar. I would have preferred to give you each $10 or $100, but I can't afford that. What I am trusting is that you will use this dollar such that its value converts into greater blessings.

This week I thought about what I could buy with a dollar—so where did I go? To the Dollar Store! There I bought a spiral notebook with 120 sheets for just a dollar, and a bottle of Elmer's Glue for just a dollar. I am giving these to the Outreach collection for school backpacks. I expect my dollars will benefit some student who will go to school better prepared to excel in learning. My currency of money will translate into the currency of wellness and truth and possibly leadership, as that student gains in self-confidence and skills.

When I got to the cash register at the Dollar Store, I was asked by the cashier if I wanted to donate a dollar to Livermore children getting ready for school. I said, "Sure," so I paid an extra dollar and the cashier took a pack of pens from one box and put it into another box of paid-for items. My visit to the Dollar Store was benefiting still another student who would have new pens to use at school. I am thinking, that student will take notes in class and complete assignments and develop relationships with his teachers. The currency of money will translate into the currency of relationship.

Now what will you use your dollar for to benefit others? Next week you will be given the opportunity to report in about your dollar bill. You'll be asked to write on a paper what you did with your dollar to keep the cycle of blessings flowing. If you will be out of town next Sunday, I invite you to e-mail me and tell me how you have used your dollar. Maybe you will invite a neighbor over for tea. (If you go out for tea or coffee, it will cost you more than a dollar!) Then you will be translating your currency of money into the currency of relationship. If the person you invite over for tea is a new friend, you will be converting your currency of money into the currency of gracious leadership too; you will be leading by example, how to cultivate a new relationship. Maybe you will spend your dollar on a note card and send it to someone who is not here today. Your currency of money will be converted into the currency of wellness. Maybe you will send the note card to someone to whom you owe an apology; then you will be converting the currency of money into the currency of truth. Or if you prefer to use the one dollar bill as a symbol for the currency of money, you may want to add to the dollar and give, say, $10 or $100 to a good cause, like to Stop Hunger Now or to Habitat for Humanity. Be creative!

The cycle of blessings all runs together. One blessing fosters another. Consider how Holy Communion is part of this cycle too, where God's blessings are converted into our holy living. Have fun with this and think about how our blessings are meant to be shared.

What project would you design and implement in order to invite the people in your church and community to understand more fully the cycle of blessings?

61

Tracking the Flow of Holy Currencies

The cycle of blessings assumes that the exchange that we initiate will return to us in some form through the cycle. In order to enable people to think about resources in this circulatory way, we must learn to track the flow of currency exchanges and, when possible, name the return even when it is only information. Three weeks after the initial invitation to invest a dollar to mobilize the cycle of blessings, the Rev. Heather Leslie Hammer reported some of the exchanges in her sermon on August 25, 2013, and invited people to continue the cycle:

> Three weeks ago I preached about "holy currencies," and I gave everyone a one dollar bill. I'd like to share a couple of the things people reported doing with their dollars:
>
> - One family added to their dollars and gave a donation to First Place for Youth, so children leaving foster care can find work and housing.
> - One person donated to find a cure for prostate cancer.
> - Another family used their money to make a dinner for friends and start a monthly tradition, they hope.
> - One person bought a silly card and a stamp and sent a wish to a young friend starting a long battle with breast cancer.
> - One person used four quarters at the Pleasanton street fair and purchased four meals for hungry children.
> - Another gave the dollar to the Pleasanton Community Counseling Center. (That's a place where people learn to stand upright, like the woman in our scripture today.)
> - One person reported: "At the Dollar Store they had wine on sale for a dollar. I couldn't decide between the sparkling pink Muscato or the Chill-Out Red, so I bought a package of 64 crayons for the schools."
>
> I hope you have been putting your dollars into the cycle of blessings. Please jot on a paper and let me know how you've spent your dollar.
>
> Oh, by the way, someone asked me what happened to the extra dollars that day. I put them into the general offering because I believe here at Lynnewood we generate blessings all the time. This is a place where day in and day out we keep the holy currencies flowing.

A year later, Lynnewood United Methodist Church created a strategic plan for 2015, which included the following goals:

Risk-Taking Mission and Service:

We plan to expand our Outreach ministries by developing ways to engage in helping low-income people in our Valley. We hope that we can cultivate a multiplying effect, such that what we do enhances others' ability to do more for themselves and for our community. We want to be directly engaged with people in poverty.

Goal 7: Work with the Vision Team and Outreach Committee to study the existing community services and needs in the Tri-Valley.

Goal 8: Develop a program offering financial education and assistance to people in poverty in the Tri-Valley.

   A. Work with Finance Committee and the UMC Conference to research and implement a program to offer micro-loans.
   B. Work with the Endowment Committee to educate our congregation about financial investment and giving.

Goal 9: Develop a program of families helping families, building relationships with low-income families in the Tri-Valley.

Lynnewood United Methodist Church had learned to think and be missional by utilizing one dollar in exchange for blessings in the community. Now they are moving in a concerted effort to flow more of their resources outward to the community—discovering the truth about needs and services there, sharing their currency of money in the form of micro-loans, and developing their currency of relationship with their program of families helping families.

The choices we make each day, even with a dollar, can have significant consequences. What exchanges are you making each day with the resources that you have? Are the exchanges flowing the resources toward blessings? How do you teach and encourage others to choose blessings and life with their resources?

I call heaven and earth to witness against you today that I have set before you life and death, blessings and curses. Choose life so that you and your descendants may live,... (Deuteronomy 30:19)

62

Beneficial Event

My earliest memory of money came from receiving 利事 (Cantonese pronunciation: Lai See) during Chinese New Year. Relatives coming to visit during the first week of the year would give red envelopes with money inside to children. The word 利, Lai, means profit or benefit. The word 事, See, means event or happening. So, 利事 can literally means beneficial event. As a young child, receiving these red envelopes certainly was a beneficial event. By the end of the week, I would have collected enough money for my annual allowance. I remembered one year my mother took me to a bank to open my first savings account with my collected share.

But there is much more to this tradition than children receiving and learning about money. The proper 利事 etiquette "requires" those who have more to give to those who have less. For example, if you are the boss, you should give 利事 to your employees. If you live in an apartment complex with a management staff, you should give 利事 to your security guard, janitors, and doorman. In other words, during the first week of the Chinese New Year, the big beneficial event is the massive movement of money from those who have more to those who have less.

Perhaps embedded in the Chinese New Year tradition is a yearning or at least a reminder to create a more sustainable community by intentionally moving our financial resources in the direction of the poor and needy. 利事 is part of the gift economy through which resources always flow toward the "empty."

Instead of waiting for this to happen once a year in communities that celebrate Chinese New Year, what if we, as a nation, start a movement of "beneficial event" every month. Once a month, everyone who "has" will give to those around them who have less. Every month, we can give a massive infusion of resources to mobilize the economy toward the holy.

63

Foolishness of God

In their book *Scarcity*, Sendhil Mullainathan and Eldar Shafir explain why the poor often make decisions that are bad for them in the long run: going to loan sharks, not saving enough, not getting their children vaccinated, or not sending their children to school. Instead of blaming the poor, they tell of the effect of "tunneling" as a result of constantly living with scarcity. We are so focused on not having enough that our brain capacity to make wise and creative decisions is diminished. They called this "bandwidth tax."

> Bandwidth measures our computational capacity, our ability to pay attention, to make good decisions, to stick with our plans, and to resist temptations. Bandwidth correlates with everything from intelligence and SAT performance to impulse control and success on diets... By constantly drawing us back into the tunnel, scarcity taxes our bandwidth and, as a result, inhibits our most fundamental capacity.[37]

According to Mullainathan and Shafir, economizing on bandwidth can yield high returns. We can provide programs for the poor in ways that increase their bandwidth so that they can make sound decisions for a sustainable future. The first step is to find ways to enter the "tunnel" and interrupt the tunneling process. For example, micro-financing by itself may not help the poor in the long run when they are tunneling. Providing a community that reminds them to pay back in small amounts every week will help them get out of the scarcity trap in the future.[38] In holy currencies terms, we need to develop our relationship currencies with the poor and issue frequent reminders, as friends, for them to do the constructive sustainable things that may be outside their tunneled minds and vision.

Programs that can increase their capacity to make sound decisions include accessible childcare, creating jobs with dependable and stable incomes, and insurance products and creative saving programs to help them build up a financial cushion so that unexpected, small financial shocks don't drive them back into the scarcity trap. "Child care provides more than just child care, and the right financial product does much more than just create

---

[37]See Sendhil Mullainathan and Eldar Shafir, *Scarcity* (New York: Picador, 2013), 41–42.
[38]I recommend reading the chapter titled, "Improving the lives of the poor." Ibid., 167–81.

savings for a rainy day. Each of these can liberate bandwidth, boost IQ, firm up self-control, enhance clarity of thinking, and even improve sleep."[39]

Christianity, to some, seems like foolishness—in a world of scarcity, why would anyone want to give up one's life for another as Jesus did? But this foolishness is actually wisdom, based on God's spirituality of abundance—there is always enough when we share what we have. Communities that practice this foolishness of giving can stop people from tunneling—obsessing over not having enough—and, therefore, increase the people's bandwidth—their ability to make wise and creative decisions that foster a sustainable future for all.

> For God's foolishness is wiser than human wisdom, and God's weakness is stronger than human strength. (1 Corinthians 1:25)

---

[39]Ibid., 180.

64

Livable Wage and Sustainable Community

One morning, I heard this story on CBS News: three waitresses at the Boone County Family Restaurant in Caledonia, Illinois, received a $15,000 tip from a woman who overheard them discussing their financial needs. Why is this news? Because being moved by compassion for others and then deciding to do something about it is rare in our world today. This is news precisely because giving to those in need is no longer part of our culture. Yet, a society where the resourceful ones don't give back is unsustainable.

While this woman offered her money to provide temporary relief for the waitresses, I would challenge us to use our talents and resources to work for a longer-term transformation of our system—helping local businesses to provide a livable wage for their workers. Instead of waiting for the government to raise the minimum wage, we can do many things right where we live, especially those of us who are part of community organizations such as churches, service clubs, and other organizations.

Go to the businesses that hire minimum wage workers in your neighborhood. Invite the owners to gather for a conversation about how the community can work together to raise the wage of the workers to a livable level. For example, if raising the minimum wage means a particular business needs to increase its customer base, can members of certain organizations make a commitment to patronize the business on a regular basis, knowing that the money they spend there will assure that the workers earn a livable wage?

Other potential solutions may include finding ways for the community to train workers so that they can increase their work capability, looking for a grant to subsidize the businesses until they are able to sustain the increased wage. When caring and resourceful people in a community come together to solve a problem, they can usually find creative solutions.

If your neighborhood becomes a place where most businesses are offering a livable wage to their workers, more hardworking people will want to live there and spend what they earn there. This, in turn, keeps resources flowing in more dynamic and healthy ways, contributing to a more sustainable local community.

65

Pledge Card for Currency of Money

Most churches are familiar with a pledge card that asks church members to commit financially in support of the church's ministries. However, in holy currencies/cycle of blessings thinking, there are many more ways to develop the currency of money beyond asking just the membership to give. In this pledge card, we also ask church members to commit to raising money from outside sources for an existing or new ministry. Depending on the ministry, people may support it financially even when they are not members of the church, if the ministry cultivates wellness in the community of which they are a part. This pledge card also invites church members to consider using their money to support the local economy, such as patronizing ethical businesses that hire local people, using local resources, and giving back to the local community. The church will not see this money in its budget, but it is good to know that, through the use of money, we are consciously supporting the local economy, fostering wellness in the community. Finally, this pledge card invites church members to give to other nonprofit organizations doing good work in the community—building trusting relationships, speaking the truth, and cultivating wellness.

When you are making a financial commitment to your church this year, be creative and add some new elements to it similar to the ones presented in this pledge card. You might start a conversation and a new trend for the people in your church to look outward, and to be missional, based on how they make their financial contributions to different kinds of ministries.

Pledge Card for Currency of Money

- I commit $ _____ for my church's ministries.
- I commit to raise $ _____ from _____ (sources outside church membership) for _____ (name of existing or new ministry).
- I commit $ _____ to support the local community economy by spending it at _____ .
- I commit $ _____ to give to other nonprofit organizations that foster wellness, truth, and trusting relationships in our local community, such as _____ .

My name: _____ My accountable person: _____

_____   _____
    signature   signature

Date: _____

66

Best Funerals in Town

One of the great joys in my ministry is to receive holy currency stories. These are reports from individuals and communities that have embraced holy currencies and the cycle of blessings, which then empowered them to incubate, launch, and implement missional and sustainable ministries. Here is one of the stories I find myself telling again and again to participants in Holy Currencies workshops. The Rev. Michael Cunningham, the rector of St. Mary's Episcopal Church in Lompoc, California, wrote this piece for my blog. My comments are in parentheses.

> While doing a weekend ministry event a couple of years ago with the Rev. Eric Law here at St. Mary's in Lompoc, we developed a response to Eric's teachings concerning missional ministry and a new way of encountering opportunities. Here is a brief description of that event...and the remarkable results.
>
> Since coming to St. Mary's in 2007, the Holy Spirit has given me the ministry of death and dying and funerals. Lots of funerals. As of this writing in August of 2013...over 100 now and counting. When our teams from St. Mary's in Lompoc and St. Peter's in Santa Maria gathered, my team discovered that the Spirit was giving us an opportunity for evangelism and growth that we had not recognized until Eric's brilliant work helped us to "see."

(One of the key activities that assisted the team to "see" was to reimagine an existing ministry, transforming it from a task-driven to a relationship-driven ministry.[40] The team from St. Mary's selected the funeral ministry, which was mostly done by the priest and the women's group that provided refreshments. The team explored what they could do to make this ministry more focused on building relationships with the guests.)

> That Saturday, the second day of the three-day event, my community wrote and developed a "gracious invitation" which was conveyed to the congregation the next day at both services, to invite members of the church to meet on Tuesday evening to discern together what the Spirit was calling us to do with regards to funerals and the ministry of radical hospitality.

---

[40]For a full description of the "From Task to Relationship" exercise, see Eric H. F. Law, *Holy Currencies* (St. Louis: Chalice Press, 2013), 25–26.

(This gracious invitation took about three hours to write.[41] It was carefully crafted to address the fear that people might have about participating in this relationship-based ministry. It also speaks the truth about what this ministry is. It also states clearly the commitment of time in exchange for gracious leadership.)

> You are invited to a gathering to help prepare for Sally's funeral
> on Tuesday 3/29 from 5:15 to 5:45.
> At this gathering we will talk about serving the larger Community
> who will be attending Sally's service.
> Specifically, we will talk about communion nametags, visitor crosses,
> and welcoming so many people to our church.
> We will talk about this as a ministry.
> We will not expect you to make a commitment to this ministry after
> only one meeting.
> This will not take more than 30 minutes of your time.
> We know that we are part of the Body of Christ—and that this is an
> opportunity for you to share the knowledge with others who really
> need to hear and know that God is with them,
> even in the most difficult times

Over 20 persons attended and gathered into teams that (a) cared for family members; (b) assisted newcomers and guests with the service; (c) worked on the particulars of a reception after the service; (d) greeted each person who came to the church at the edge of the patio and remained with them to the door of the church; (e) assisted the priest with the service; and (f) set up and cleaned up before and after. The funeral that all were working on was two days after the Tuesday night gathering and had over 300 persons in attendance.

Since that vanguard moment in the life of our congregation, we have had many, many more funerals...and each one has been assisted by members of the congregation, including about 14 of the original 23 [who attended that first meeting], but now added to by many others as part of the ongoing work of ministry in this place.

The Daughters of the King, a lay-order of women dedicated to prayer and support for the clergy of an Episcopal Parish, have taken on the ministry of caring for the family, but all other aspects of the

---

[41]The process of writing a gracious invitation is based on the "grace margin" concept I first presented in *Inclusion*. For a full description of how to write a gracious invitation, see Law, *Holy Currencies*, 97–102.

original identified ministry, including issuing "gracious invitations," have remained the work of the laity of the church.

St. Mary's has grown from the 120 or so persons who attended in 2007 when I first got here to over 450 as of this writing. Average Sunday attendance hovers around 160 to 180 with large occasions, Christmas and Easter and Pentecost, averaging close to 500. "Holy Currency," and the terminology of Eric's work, has become part of the lexicon here at St. Mary's...and the working understanding that we are living in a Grace Margin and evaluating decisions we make in terms of what sort of Holy Currency we are employing for each opportunity the Spirit gives us is now how we do things here.

I have known and worked with Eric for over 17 years now and can say with great conviction that his work is visionary and life-changing. Much of the work we have done together defines how I view congregational development, but none more exciting than Holy Currencies.

67

Yoga in Spanish

In 2009, St Peter's Episcopal Church, Santa Maria, was approached by the Marian Hospital to provide space for their Marian Community Education programs. In particular, they needed a place for a yoga class taught in Spanish. The Rev. Deborah Dunn, the rector of St. Peter's, apologized for the space they requested—the parish hall—because it was not in the best of shape. The floor of the parish hall was squeaky and covered with horrible blue carpet. But the director of the program insisted that it was all right—all they needed was the space.

So Deborah brought this request to the vestry (the Episcopal term for a church council or board) and the first reaction was, "Why can't we have the classes in English?"

The gentle response from Deborah: "Because this is what was proposed to us."

"Do we have to give them a key?" was the next question. Apparently, leaders of the church had not yet fully adopted missional thinking.

After some discussion, the vestry decided to accept this request because this program fit their mission to the neighborhood. They did decide to give their guests a key. Members of the vestry then began the process of making the building nicer and eventually developed a policy for building usage when and if more people in the neighborhood asked to use their space.

In 2010, St. Peter's participated in a three-day Missional Ministries in the Grace Margin training that I conducted. The holy currencies concept provided a language for them to understand what they had begun doing. One of the training activities invited them to explore how they could build relationships with the people using their facility, beyond just giving them the key. I remember telling them, "You don't need to speak Spanish to do yoga." As part of the training, they also wrote the following gracious invitation to invite church members to come for a meeting:

> You are invited to OPENING DOORS
> Sunday 9:30 to 10:30
> Brunch provided in Parke Hall
> **We will**
> Learn about the Spanish Yoga Class
> Explore possibilities to be better hosts and facilitate class meetings
> Take time to get to know more about the people
> **We will not**
> Require a long-term commitment
> Make you learn Spanish in one night
> Entice you to participate in the class
> "Whatever you did for the least of these you did for me"

Apparently, the invitation worked. Some of the church members found the courage to show up at yoga class and got to know the yoga teacher, Esther, and the Spanish-speaking community members. This was the seed for missional ministries at St. Peter's. Through these relationships, they discovered more truth about the community's needs. They now have a food bank every Thursday. They provide sack lunches. They have classes on chronic disease management.

One day, Esther, the Spanish yoga teacher, handed Deborah an envelope with money in it. Puzzled, Deborah asked what this was for. Esther said that the yoga class had decided to take up a weekly collection to start a fund for fixing the floor of the parish hall. A few weeks later, while Esther was giving Deborah the weekly collection, an "angel" of St. Peter's saw the transaction and inquired about it. (According to St. Peter's, an "angel" is someone who gives money to the church but doesn't want to be identified.) Deborah recalled the woman asking, "How much do you need to put in a new floor?"

Deborah went to a local flooring company, the owner of which was a friend of a contractor the church had used—three degrees of influence at work. He had heard about the great ministry at St. Peter's, especially the Thursday food programs. He said that a floor this size would normally cost $30,000, but the church could have it for $15,000. Why? There was a cancelled order and if she didn't mind the color and wood choice, she could have it.

So, Deborah went back to the "angel" and told her the good news. The woman pulled out her checkbook and wrote a check. Deborah noticed it was for $30,000. She said, "I think you misheard me. We only need $15,000."

The woman said, "Don't you need a new kitchen and new light fixtures too?"

When I visited St. Peter's in 2012, Deborah and the church leaders proudly showed me their new floor and, more importantly, all the ministry activities that happened in this space throughout the week.

Most churches have the asset of space, but many only use it to exchange for rent money. St. Peter's went beyond this commodity exchange and crossed a boundary to build relationships with the people from the neighborhood. The relationship currency then exchanged into truth, wellness, leadership, and more of the currency of money, which in turn increased the currency of the place.

If your church rents out spaces for groups in the community, are these just landlord-renter arrangements? If so, in what ways can you transform these arrangements into trusting, mutually supportive relationships? Building these relationships is the first step toward becoming missional. The exchanges that follow may surprise you. The return of currencies will sustain further ministries that you might not have imagined.

Do not neglect to show hospitality to strangers, for by doing that some have entertained angels without knowing it. (Hebrews 13:2)

68

Currencies Flow at the BBQ

A team of church leaders from Humber Valley United Church (HVUC), Toronto, has been participating in a year-long Holy Currencies training program. Before the summer, the team learned to write a "gracious invitation" to invite people from the neighborhood to come to their annual barbecue as an initial effort to build up their currency of relationship.

> You are invited
> To a "Friendly Community" all-ages BBQ
> To Kick off the Fall Season
> at Humber Valley United Church
> On Sept. 14, 2014, from 11:30 to 1:30 p.m.
> BBQ and activities both inside "Steed Hall" and outside on the lawn.
>
> *******************
>
> At this BBQ we will share our hospitality, our appreciation, and our friendship as we enter into a new year together as partners and neighbours in Humber Valley Village and environs. We will share lunch, enjoy some old-fashioned games, and tell stories about our lives and times in Humber Valley. HVUC will not recruit new members nor indoctrinate in any way, but we will provide ample opportunity for getting to know each other better. We hope to enhance our relationship around this building and within this wonderful community.
>
> Humber Valley United Church
> 76 Anglesey Blvd.
> "The Friendly Community Church"

At a previous church service, church members were asked to identify five people in the neighborhood whom, although not members of the church, they are thankful to know. When the invitation was completed, church members were given five invitations to hand out to the friends they had identified. In addition, they also invited the renters of their facilities and some even bravely went door-to-door inviting their neighbors. As a result, over 50 people who had never stepped foot on the church ground before, came and had a great time. Here is the article written by Donna McCorquodale and published in the October issue of Humber Valley United Church's newsletter, reporting on the success of the event:

"Congratulations!"

"What a success!"

"I had my concerns, but it all turned out great!"

Many people approached me after the Fall BBQ with these words! Thank you, one and all, for working with me on making another whacky idea into a success story. Here is what happened. The word "currency" stems from the same Latin derivative as the word "current." It means "to flow." Without flow there can be no life and our faith will wither on the vine. If we stop putting up obstacles to the expression of our faith, it will flow. So we put our faith outside on the front lawn and opened our doors wide. We delivered personal invitations. We went door to door. We reached out into the community.

During the BBQ "things" flowed. People talked to people. People met new people. The Director of Mom Net met Diana Pace of the Hillside Montessori School. They needed to talk. One of the representatives of the Camera Club asked Carolyn Whiteside if they could take photos at the Fashion Show and the Vintage Sale. Representatives of Nels Christansen's campaign party talked with me about the dearth of restaurants and gym facilities in central Etobicoke. Ideas flowed. The Camera Club representatives were interested to hear about the speaker at our Conference who specializes in using photography in worship. Perhaps they will ask them to speak to their group. We sat down with members of our friends from the True Light Korean Church and got to know each other. Relationships grew.

We had enough food. The sun shone bright and clear on a perfect early fall day. People invited other people to come to our church with no motive other than to express their gratitude. Jesus did not send forth his disciples to "recruit members for the church" but to love one another as he loves us. Straight and simple. We put tables and balloons and a giant bouncy dog on the front lawn. We opened our arms wide. And people came in; children played and ran around. People talked and talked; they ate big long hot dogs and delectable field-fresh corn from Saturday's Civic Centre Market. The community came to the church. We celebrated our blessings together, all together. Let this be a new beginning of ministry, not just to ourselves but to our community. We will demonstrate our Christian faith and we will grow. If you missed this one, don't worry. There will be more.

69

I Know a Good Thing When I See One

The Life Enrichment Center (LEC) began as the Back Door grocery ministry of the Dayton (Ohio) Vineyard Church. In 2002, it became an independent 501(c)3 nonprofit and relocated to Erwin Street in East Dayton. Within a few years, the ministry had outgrown the Erwin Street space. Jeff Sorrell, the founder and executive director, noticed there was a 57,000 square foot building on 4.5 acres with a service garage that had been standing empty for at least two years. Jeff found out that the owner, John Staten, wanted to sell. Jeff brought with him the building floor plan, in which he put information on how the ministries of LEC would work in the facility. These ministries included meals and supplemental groceries, building community, educational offerings, health and wellness, resources and referrals, a bike shop, and a child safety village. By the time Jeff finished telling the LEC story, John Staten was convinced that this ministry was worth supporting. Jeff recalled John saying, "I know a good idea when I see one."

John then offered the following deal to Jeff: The LEC could lease the building with the option to buy it, at $12,000 per month plus $92,000 per year of utility cost. Jeff took it to the LEC board and the board returned with the following counter-offer: The LEC would pay $500 per month (this is not a typo, it really was $500), with the option to buy. The lease would go up to $1,000 the second year, $2,000 the third, $4,000 the fourth, and $8,000 the fifth. Of course, LEC would pay all utilities. Even though the building's value was assessed at $850,000, the LEC offered to buy the building at the price of $550,000.

Now, you would think, no owner in his right mind would accept this offer! But to everybody's surprise, John Staten not only accepted the offer, he also pledged to give LEC $60,000 per year, accumulating to $300,000 in five years.

When I tell people this story, the first reaction is always disbelief. This story is unbelievable if we only focus on the money involved in this exchange. But the story is not really about money. It is about the relationship built between Jeff and John. Through this relationship, Jeff told the truth about the needs of the people in Dayton and stirred up the passion in John to foster wellness in his community. As a result, he invested his money and property toward housing the Life Enrichment Center and trusting in the gracious leadership of Jeff and his staff to implement all the wellness programs.

In 2008, after extensive renovations, the Life Enrichment Center opened in its current home at 425 N. Findlay Street. In 2015, when I talked with Jeff, the Life Enrichment Center was hoping to do a major fundraiser to pay off the building that year.

If you have a ministry idea and are looking for a place to house it, don't let money stop you from fully exploring the possibilities. Look around your neighborhood. Do you see any buildings that are not being used? A place that is not being used is not worth anything. It ceases to be a currency. What ministries would you put in these places? Do you know the owners? How would you build a relationship with the owners to explore potential ministry exchanges?

> As for those who in the present age are rich, command them not to be haughty, or to set their hopes on the uncertainty of riches, but rather on God who richly provides us with everything for our enjoyment. They are to do good, to be rich in good works, generous, and ready to share, thus storing up for themselves the treasure of a good foundation for the future, so that they may take hold of the life that really is life. (1 Timothy 6:17–19)

70

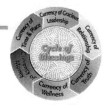

GracEconomics Food Co-Op

I was invited to offer a Holy Currencies workshop at St. Paul's Episcopal Church in Bakersfield, California, in 2014. Upon arrival, Alison and Jason introduced themselves as the founders and coordinators of the church's Food Pantry Co-Op ministry. I was told that the Co-Op was built upon the GracEconomics concept I taught at an earlier workshop for the Episcopal Diocese of San Joaquin, of which St. Paul's was one of the participating churches. While they were giving me the tour, a person came in to inquire about the food program. Alison sat down with her at the computer and began to set up a profile of her needs. She asked the woman about the number of people in her household. What were their ages? Did any member of her family have any dietary issues or special needs? In the process, they developed a relationship. This new ministry not only practices GracEconomics, it also mobilizes the currencies of relationship, wellness, gracious leadership, and time and place. I will let the information on the church's website speak for itself:[42]

St. Paul's CO-OP
Sundays, 1:00 – 3:00 P.M.
Thursdays, 9:30 A.M. – 12:30 P.M.

Our goal is to empower our customers based on shared responsibility, mutual support, and accountability through the process of exchange rather than simply offering one-way giving. Customers have two options to participate in either our Buying Club or Work Program.

We offer groceries, fresh produce grown from local farmers, socks, shoes, underwear, dog food, cat food, baby food, diapers, and toiletries every Sunday and Thursday. The Thrift Shop is open every Sunday during distribution hours.

Dues are $5.00, $3.00, and $1.00, or 90, 60, or 30 minutes of your time for each total transaction. Members may receive produce twice a week and groceries and clothing once a week. Every dollar earned from the Buying Club Dues is directly turned around into buying more items for the CO-OP distribution.

---

[42]Go the St. Paul's website to learn the latest information of the Food Co-Op ministry at http://www.stpaulsepiscopalbakersfield.org/st-pauls-co-op.html.

The Work Program allows the opportunity to earn groceries and produce through any type of work accomplished through physical needs of St. Paul's Episcopal Church and the St. Paul's CO-OP. The Work Program participants will tend to duties such as distribution in both the Thrift Shop and the Food Pantry, collection of produce, sorting through donations, accounting, recipe writing and distribution, sweeping the grounds or parking lots, tending to the flower beds, and assisting in P.R. efforts.

The St. Paul's CO-OP opened February 23, 2014, responding to Jesus' command to feed his sheep in both spiritual and physical manners. The CO-OP foundation was inspired by *Toxic Charity* by Robert Lupton and *Holy Currencies* by Eric Law. The St. Paul's CO-OP has members rather than customers. **Our primary rules are that every individual involved is treated with the dignity and respect they deserve as children of God and that all needs capable of being met are attended to.** Thus far, this model is working out. The S.P.C. has proudly served 135 members over 335 transactions and steadily increases every week.

Our members range from students, grandparents raising younger generations, elderly and disabled sacrificing food for medications and housing, homeless who have been discarded by society, and gainfully employed individuals who, despite their best efforts, still face food insecurity.

Instead of taking the pamphlet preaching approach at evangelism, trying to shove who God is into a 5 minute platform speech, we strive to live it. **Our members experience our care and love for them, trust they will be treated with dignity, and know there are expectations for them. We are not tossing bags of food into the streets and ignoring the causations for homelessness and poverty.** The CO-OP is building a community that is centered with a concept that God is too big to be summed up in a few minutes and must be implemented in daily life to prove that we are who we claim to be. This has created more conversation and moments of grace than ever imagined because our members feel safe, appreciated, and loved; for all are truly welcome at God's table. It is a rarity that a member comes in and does not sit to engage in conversation, even if it is about life's most trivial aspects. It is humbling to see the astounding number of God's children and neighbors who do not feel loved or worthwhile to anyone, especially themselves. We strive to ensure all members know how precious they are and that the S.P.C. will assist however possible so that they live the bountiful life they deserve. This tremendous need is what drives us to operate and feed his sheep to our greatest capacity.

When they had finished breakfast, Jesus said to Simon Peter, "Simon son of John, do you love me more than these?" He said to him, "Yes, Lord; you know that I love you." Jesus said to him, "Feed my lambs." (John 21:15)

71

GracEconomics Grocery Store

New ideas of missional and sustainable ministries always emerge during the Holy Currencies workshops I have facilitated in the last several years. Many of these ideas have come from an exercise in which we invite participants to reimagine a ministry being transformed from a linear, doing-for, charity model into a spiral, relationship-building, reciprocal form. These new ideas are always met with excitement. Some of these ideas have not yet been realized, but I want to share them anyway. Maybe you will be inspired to make them real.

Many churches and community centers have food pantries, which are often run in a linear, goal-driven fashion. That is, we take in the food donations, put them in bags with volunteers, line up the recipients, hand them the bags of food, clean up, and we are done for the day. This linear approach is not sustainable in number of ways:

1. It relies solely on donations of food and money. If for some reason the sources of donated food and money run dry, this ministry would cease.
2. It does not ask the receivers for anything in return. By maintaining the one-way giver-receiver relationship, we might not be valuing the integrity and dignity of the receivers.
3. The receivers have no choice in what food items they receive. This reinforces the powerlessness of the receivers.

What if we were to transform a food pantry into a GracEconomics Grocery Store? Using the available space, we could build a store that looks and feels like a regular neighborhood grocery store. The only difference is that there would be no price tags and stickers on the food items. This store would stock the basics—daily essential items such as milk, eggs, juice, etc., as well as seasonal and donated food. The store would be a place where both the ones who have money and the ones who have no money would feel comfortable coming in and "shopping." Everyone would be welcome to come in and select from the shelves any items that he or she needs for self and family. At the checkout counter, if you have money, you can make a donation; if you don't, you can fill out a card to offer other kind of currencies in exchange, such as volunteering to work at the store for a few hours if you have the time, or offering your talents in ways that are appropriate.

The GracEoncomics Grocery serves the same function as a linear, traditional church food program in providing food for the poor, but it does much more. It can become a gathering place where those who have and those who have not can "shop" side-by-side. Those who have money and resources will know where their donation will be used to keep this ministry financially sustainable. Those who have not are treated with respect, and feel they are valued because they can take part in contributing to the ministry and the community.

As we were exploring this idea at a seminary, a graduating, soon-to-be-ordained student came up with another idea to develop the currencies of relationship further. She said she would invite members of her church to be "personal shoppers" at such a store. That is, when someone walked in, he or she would be greeted by a personal shopper who took the time to find out more about his or her family: how many people are being fed, and what are their ages? The personal shopper would direct the guest to the appropriate shelves stocked with delicious and healthy items. If the shopper did not know how to prepare a certain food item, the personal shopper would be equipped with knowledge to show him or her how to do that.

So here is the basic idea. I believe such a ministry can be self-sustaining financially with the donations from the shoppers who have money. Combined with the hours from volunteers, the cost of running such an operation would be minimal. This is missional because there are many opportunities for building relationships. If you decide to try this by either converting your food pantry ministry or creating a new GracEconomics Grocery Store, please let me know. The Kaleidoscope Institute would love to assist, document, and share your experience. Imagine what it would be like if every church situated at the crossroads of rich and poor neighborhoods had a GracEconomics Grocery Store.

72

GracEconomics Exchange Center

I was in a thrift store the other day and found a beautiful tie. I would have paid at least $10 for it, but the thrift shop priced it at only $3. So I paid $3. As I was leaving the store, I realized that the idea of a thrift store can be expanded into a more missional and sustainable ministry.

Many churches and community organizations have thrift stores for the purpose of fundraising. Most thrift stores are conceived and operated using a charity model. That is, people donate goods to the store, shoppers pay a modest price for these items, and the money collected goes to the charities or ministries that the thrift store supports.

What if we transformed the thrift store into a GracEconomics Exchange Center? Here is how it might work: The store would continue to receive donated goods. If possible, the donors of items would be asked to provide an estimate of what each item is worth. Each item is priced in the range between $0 and the estimated monetary price. A shopper could pay any amount within that range. This way, those who can afford it may pay at a higher rate, while those who have little or no financial resources can have the item free-of-charge. In any case, the shoppers would then be asked to consider other ways to contribute to the ministry in exchange for the items they receive. This could be done by asking them to fill out a card to describe their offering in currencies other than money. For example, someone might offer to volunteer at the store for an hour. Depending on the gifts and talents of the shopper, he or she might offer, for example, to clean someone's house, or to custom-knit a sweater for someone, which could be valued at a certain amount of money. These cards of offering would then be posted on a bulletin board in the store. A shopper might decide to "buy" the custom-knit sweater or the cleaning service with money, which would go to support the ministry, or he or she might pay with other currencies by filling out another card.

This ministry is missional because it provides opportunities for the people who run the ministry to build relationships with the shoppers. Also, the shoppers are getting to know each other in the process of exchanging goods, time, treasures, and talent. This ministry is sustainable because the shoppers who can afford to pay with money at the higher range would offset the cost for those who receive the goods free, and should provide enough monetary income to pay for the cost of running such a ministry.

Once the people in the community figured out how the GracEconomics Exchange Center worked, they might even discover other innovative exchanges that could contribute to creating a sustainable community together.

73

GracEconomics Advance Fund

Many people live from paycheck to paycheck with little financial room to maneuver. An unexpected emergency or event requiring money would send them into the scarcity trap. They might seek short-term fixes such as so-called payday loans, which charge an enormous amount of interest and fees, resulting in borrowers falling deeper into debt.

During a Holy Currencies workshop, a group came up with the idea of a GracEonomics Advance Fund. Church members could pool their financial resources to create a fund. The fund would give people emergency loans with no interest and flexible repayment terms. Instead of paying interest, recipients of a loan from the GracEconomics Advance Fund would agree to attend financial management classes provided by the church. Aside from learning ways to manage one's finances, participants would form a supportive community with each other and with members of the church. Through this network, participants would also share the truth of their experiences, find creative ways to address concerns, determine a payment plan to replenish the fund, and foster a realistic vision of a sustainable future for themselves and their families.

A Roman Catholic Church with close to 10,000 members discovered that many people in their neighborhood were about to be evicted because they were behind on their rent payments. I challenged the leaders of the church to create an "emergency rent fund" for their neighbors. "Where is the money coming from?" was the question. I said, "If each member of the church gives one dollar to this fund, you would have $10,000 to start this ministry, and $10,000 can cover a lot of rent." Once the tenants received the temporary relief, the church could help create a truth event inviting the landlords and tenants to come together for constructive dialogue.

In what ways can your church community mobilize your currencies of money to create opportunities for developing currencies of relationship and truth, and fostering wellness throughout the community?

74

Race Together at Starbucks

For a week in March 2015 when you went to Starbucks to buy a drink, the baristas would scribble "Race Together" on your cup as a way to encourage you to start a conversation about race relations. I was curious, excited, and cautious about this movement. I was also saddened by the withdrawal of this plan by Starbucks a week later after receiving controversial responses.

With my curiosity, I went to the Internet in search of the mission of Starbucks, and here is what I found:

Our Mission:
To inspire and nurture the human spirit—one person, one cup and one neighborhood at a time.

Our Values:
With our partners, our coffee and our customers at our core, we live these values:

- Creating a culture of warmth and belonging, where everyone is welcome.
- Acting with courage, challenging the status quo and finding new ways to grow our company and each other.
- Being present, connecting with transparency, dignity and respect.
- Delivering our very best in all we do, holding ourselves accountable for results.
- We are performance drive, through the lens of humanity.

It made sense for a company with this mission and these values to make such a bold and controversial move. I was excited because I saw a great potential for Starbucks "to nurture and inspire the human spirit" in its 12,000 locations across the United States.

However, I was cautious and concerned about whether the Starbucks employees and customers had the gracious leadership skills to create "a culture of warmth and belonging where everyone is welcome" to engage in this dialogue on race with "courage," "dignity and respect" and with accountability.

Having been involved in interracial dialogue work since the 1980s, I know that to create respectful environments that foster constructive conversations about difficult topics does not happen simply because we want it to happen. It takes intentional efforts, combined with gracious leadership skills, to foster such an environment for truth speaking.

Even though Starbucks pulled the plug on this initiative, I still want to support the spirit of what Starbucks wanted to do in an effort to live out its mission. So I challenge you to consider the following:

1. Go to your neighborhood Starbucks and propose to set up a space, perhaps a circle of five or six chairs in the store, designated as the "Race Together Place."
2. Offer to be the facilitator at least for one hour a day for three days a week.
3. Put up a sign inviting people to join the group.
   Interested people would be invited to read and sign the following commitment statement before joining the conversation:

I,_____, am interested in participating in a constructive dialogue on race relations and

- I will share my own story
- I will be curious and listen to others' stories
- I will ask clarifying questions, and not debate who is right or wrong
- I will seek to understand
- I will not interrupt, judge, or disparage
- and I know it is okay to be angry but will not use my anger to hurt others.

_____   _____
signature   date

---

4. At each session, there could be a topic for dialogue. Here are some possibilities:
   a. If I have to say who I am racially, I would say I am...
   b. As a person of my racial background, one advantage I have is...
   c. As a person of my racial background, one challenge I face is...
   d. Recall an earlier experience in which you learned that skin color differences could be a positive thing. Recall an earlier experience in which you learned that skin color differences could be a negative thing. Share your stories and listen to others.

75

As the Waters Cover the Sea

As the Waters Cover the Sea

I pray for a world one day
Where no one needs to be afraid:
A world that's full of the knowledge of peace
As the waters cover the sea
As the waters cover the sea.
Then the calf and the lion shall eat straw together.
The cow and the bear shall peacefully graze.
Their young shall lie down next to each other.
In their midst, a little child at play.
Then the wolf and the lamb shall live together.
The leopard and the kid; the fierce and the small;
And they'll all dwell in harmony together
And a little child shall lead them all.
Fill me with your love, O God.
Pour your justice over me.
Flood me with your power to forgive
And soak me in your peace
As the waters cover the sea.
(Inspired by Isaiah 11:6–9)

As the Waters Cover the Sea

Verses

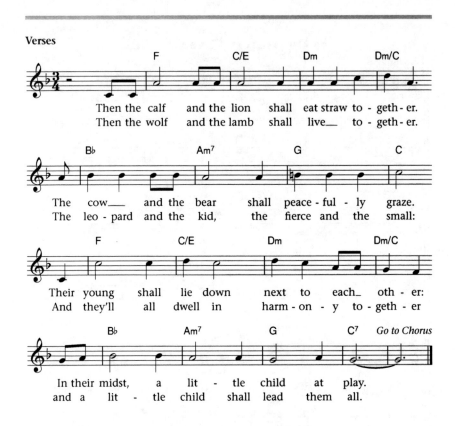

Then the calf and the lion shall eat straw to-geth-er.
Then the wolf and the lamb shall live__ to-geth-er.

The cow__ and the bear shall peace-ful-ly graze.
The leo-pard and the kid, the fierce and the small:

Their young shall lie down next to each__ oth-er:
And they'll all dwell in harm-on-y to-geth-er

In their midst, a lit-tle child at play.
and a lit-tle child shall lead them all.

To be sung simultaneously with the chorus.

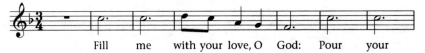

Fill me with your love, O God: Pour your

jus-tice o-ver me. Flood me with the pow-er to for-give and soak me

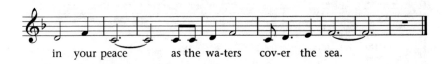

in your peace as the wa-ters cov-er the sea.

76

Lady in the Alley

"There's an area near our center that used to be the place where sex workers brought their customers," Maria Rodriguez-Winter shared during a dinner gathering with United Methodist church leaders in Toledo. "So we decided to paint a mural that has in it the Ten Commandments and the image of Our Lady of Guadalupe. And the sexual activity stopped. Instead, people would stop by the alley and pray and make the sign of the cross."

Maria is the executive director of the Sofia Quintero Art and Cultural Center in Toledo, Ohio.[43] Part of the mission of the center is to support and give "voice to the artistic and educational expressions which advance community development, responsibility and social equity, cultural diversity, global awareness and stewardship, as well as the empowerment of the Latina and Latino Identities."[44]

On the way to the dinner gathering, Tom, a United Methodist pastor, insisted that we drive by the center. I saw the beautiful murals and glass art sculptures amidst the "resting" gardens (it was winter). The center had six community gardens that offered community members a way to participate in organic gardening, year-round art programs to express themselves, and opportunities for youth from low-income families to learn hands-on skills in carpentry and painting. But the most important thing for me was to see how this center, led by Maria, reclaimed the land and buildings in the middle of an ignored and under-supported neighborhood, and created a safe space for the people to strengthen their identity and express themselves. This is a great example of developing the currency of place through the arts, which functions like a ladder between the holy and the unholy, transforming a place of abuse, exploitation, and oppression into a place for beauty, hope, and prayers.

So take a look around your neighborhood. Where are the ignored, discarded, and dangerous places? How can you and your organizations reclaim these places and turn them into useful currencies—places that support, nurture, and nourish the people in the community?

> [Jacob] came to a certain place and stayed there for the night, because the sun had set. Taking one of the stones of the place, he put it under his head and lay down in that place. And he dreamed

---

[43]See www.sqacc.org for the latest information on Sofia Quintero Art and Cultural Center.

[44]From Mission Statement on About Us page of www.sqacc.org.

that there was a ladder set up on the earth, the top of it reaching to heaven; and the angels of God were ascending and descending on it... Then Jacob woke from his sleep and said, "Surely the Lord is in this place—and I did not know it!" (Genesis 28:11–12, 16)

77

Pledge Card for Currency of Place

When assessing the currency of place, most churches tend to confine their thinking to the buildings and grounds of the church. Of course, it is important to explore more ways for churches to share their own spaces with the neighborhood, exchanging for leadership, wellness, relationship, and even money. However, there is more to currency of place if we only look outward. For example, church members' homes can be made available for different kinds of ministries—home church, prayer groups, Bible study group, community meetings, fundraisers. There are public spaces we can access for all kind of ministries. There are businesses with spaces that we can negotiate to use for ministries. Like our friend Jeff Sorrell of the Life Enrichment Center in Dayton, Ohio, we can reach out to owners of properties and speak the truth, in order to access more places for ministries. We can even reclaim places that have been neglected and transform them into places for wellness. So the pledge card for currency of place invites church members to be creative in finding the places they own and the places to which they have access, such as their businesses, and public spaces for existing and new ministries.

Make a list of places to which you have access. What ministries might work in these places? Then make a pledge.

Pledge Card for Currency of Place

- I commit to renovate/beautify/refurbish _____ (location of church property) for _____ (name of existing or new ministry).
- I commit _____ (location I own) for _____ (name of existing or new ministry); and
- I commit to making _____ (location to which I have access) available for _____ (name of existing or new ministry).

My name: _____ My accountable person: _____

_____   _____
    signature   signature

Date: _____

78

Art and Community Transformation

After an intensive weekend workshop with a group of church leaders in the Philadelphia area, I realized I had a free morning before I would fly back home. I suggested to my friend and host, the Rev. Kathy Walker, that we go and see an artist's masterpiece that transformed a North Philadelphia neighborhood facing poverty, crime, pollution, and social alienation. Ever since I watched the video of the artist, Lily Yeh, giving a presentation at the 2009 Bioneer Conference, I had wanted to see for myself the Village of Arts and Humanities.[45]

We got in the car and began making our way on Germantown Avenue through the different neighborhoods—from the most affluent to the poorest, from mansions to boarded-up buildings. Each neighborhood has its own historical landmarks. Just as we were beginning to wonder where this work of art was, we saw a whole block of buildings painted with multi-colored horizontal stripes—not one building, but the whole block. Surely, this took a lot of work getting all the building owners to agree to make their buildings one giant canvas. Then we saw the first Mosaic garden that Lily and the children in the neighborhood had shaped with their own hands.

In 1989, while guiding a tour group of visiting Chinese artists around Philadelphia, Lily Yeh brought them to the studio of dancer Arthur Hall in North Philadelphia. Arthur asked her for help in reviving a particularly grim stretch of the neighborhood outside. Lily was shocked at the state of the streets—vacant lots, boarded-up buildings, rubble and trash everywhere. Lily began gathering up the trash, which drew the attention of local kids wanting to know, she recalled, what "this crazy Chinese lady" was up to. Soon their parents were watching too, and Yeh realized she had some collaborators for what was to be the most important art project of her life. Soon everyone was involved in cleaning up the area, painting murals, and creating an "art park," which became the pride of the community.

More than 25 years later, the small art park Lily and a group of neighborhood kids started has grown into a tangible symbol of renewal known as the Village of Arts and Humanities. The village covers more than 120 formerly vacant lots with murals, numerous sculpture gardens, mosaics, parks, community gardens, playgrounds, performance spaces, basketball courts, neighborhood art studios, and even a tree farm.

---

[45]See the video at https://www.youtube.com/watch?v=nTvtI37JhBw. It also includes the fantastic work that Lily Yeh later did in Rwanda.

After immersing ourselves in the various parts of the village—angels watching over the neighborhood; saints guarding a memorial to those who died; sparkling benches for rest and meditation; a glorious tree of life; wild creatures made out of a tree trunk, a rock, or fallen tree—we entered the office of the Village of Arts and Humanities and were embraced by Brenda Toler, the administrative manager. Inside, we found a dance studio, along with spaces for art classes, writing classes, and pottery-making. Brenda told us her grandchildren were the first to work with Lily. She gave us books and magazines documenting the projects they did with artists and especially the young people in the neighborhood. We left with smiles on our faces, knowing that the dream of sustainable community is possible when we can be artist-leaders like Lily Yeh. For her, being an artist "is not just about making art... It is about delivering the vision one is given...and about doing the right thing without sparing oneself."[46]

Lily describes her calling this way: "When I see brokenness, poverty and crime in inner cities, I also see the enormous potential and readiness for transformation and rebirth. We are creating an art form that comes from the heart and reflects the pain and sorrow of people's lives. It also expresses joy, beauty and love. This process lays the foundation of building a genuine community in which people are reconnected with their families, sustained by meaningful work, nurtured by the care of each other and will together raise and educate their children. Then we witness social change in action."[47]

---

[46]From her biography at the Project for Public Spaces website: http://www.pps.org/reference/lyeh/.

[47]Most of the information about Lily Yeh and the Village of Arts and Humanities comes from the Project for Public Spaces website: http://www.pps.org/reference/lyeh/.

79

Make Us Instruments of Your Peace

Make us instruments of your peace.
Where there's hatred, let us sow love.
Where there's injury, let us pardon.
Where there's discord, bring us union.
Where there doubt, let us sow faith.
Where there's darkness, let us be light.
Where there's sadness, let us bring joy.
Where there's despair, let us sow hope.
Make us instruments of your peace.
It's in giving that we receive;
It's in pardoning that we are pardoned;
It's in dying that we are born to eternal life.
(Inspired by the peace prayer of St. Francis.)

Make Us Instruments of Your Peace

Canon I

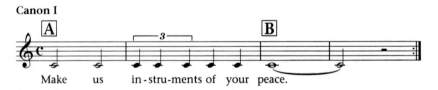

Make us in-stru-ments of your peace.

Canon IV

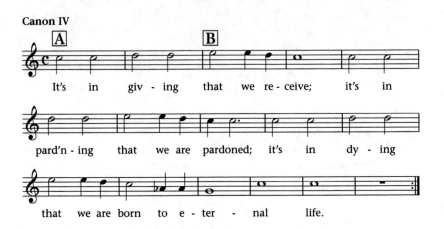

It's in giv - ing that we re - ceive; it's in

pard'n - ing that we are pardoned; it's in dy - ing

that we are born to e - ter - nal life.

Accompaniment

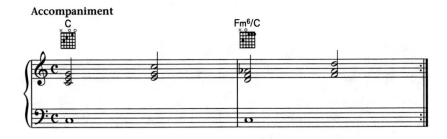

80

Artist-Leader

As a writer, sometimes I have come up with ideas that the conventional English language did not have existing words to describe. So I created new words or terms by connecting words that had not been coupled or combined before. Here are some examples of coupling of words (some hypenated, some not) that I have used: "Grace Margin," "Holy Currencies," Waste=Resource, "Network Globally, Connect Locally," Ancient-Future-Now, Artist-Leader, Sustainist, and GracEconomics. The presence of hyphenated words and intentional coupling of previously unrelated words are indications of the emergence of something new—a concept, idea, identity, experience, organization, or community that is so novel, we need a new word or phrase to describe it.

Matthew Fox, in his classic book *A Spirituality Named Compassion and the Healing of the Global Village, Humpty Dumpty and Us,* writes, "The very heart of being creative is seeing relations between matter and form that no one has ever imagined before or that people deeply want and need to see."[48] This ability to make connections is the essence of being an artist.

Jesus was an artist-leader in that he connected the concept of "messiah" with suffering, dying, and giving up of himself for others. When he spoke of these connections, even his friends were not able to accept what he was saying until the whole gospel story was lived out. This is the risk that an artist-leader takes.

Gracious leaders are artist-leaders. We see connections where there seem to be none. We discover resources in the most unlikely places and then connect them with unlikely recipients. Such ideas seem outrageous for some and downright dangerous for others.

Bill Strickland, Jeff Sorrell, Maria Rodriguez-Winter, and Lily Yeh are all artist-leaders who make connections with people and resources, creating sustainable communities. The people I named in my last book—Gregory Boyle, Terry Waite, Muhammad Yunus, Philbert Kalisa, and Jon Bon Jovi— are all artist-leaders. There are many others I am not able to include in this book. For example, take a look at the Rev. Becca Stevens, an Episcopal priest who created Magdalene, a residential program for women who have survived lives of prostitution, trafficking, addiction, and life on the streets. In order to make this ministry sustainable, she also founded a social enterprise called

---

[48]See Matthew Fox, *A Spirituality Named Compassion and the Healing of the Global Village, Humpty Dumpty and Us* (Minneapolis: Winston Press, 1979), 127.

Thistle Farms, which is run by the women of Magdalene.[49] You can find Thistle Farms products in over 400 stores in Tennessee and across the country.

Another example is Mason Wartman, the owner of Rosa's Fresh Pizza.[50] He asks his customers to give an extra dollar in exchange for a Post-It® note on which the customer can write a message. These notes are then posted on the wall of the restaurant. When someone who doesn't have money comes in, he or she can just take one of the notes in exchange for a slice of pizza. There are thousands of post-it notes (currency) on the wall of Rosa's Fresh Pizza.

When we live the cycle of blessings and adopt a holy currency mindset, making connections comes naturally. The constant question, "What blessings can this resource exchange into?" becomes the creative moment when new connections, new exchanges, and new flows are conceived, making us artist-leaders.

---

[49]You can learn more about Becca Stevers at http://www.beccastevens.org/ and this Thistle Farms at http://www.thistlefarms.org/.

[50]Find more information about Rosa's Fresh Pizza at http://www.nbcphiladelphia.com/entertainment/the-scene/Rosas-Pizza-Ellen-288448131.html.

81

Taking the Church Out to the World

I believe everyone can be an artist-leader. I have designed activities to help people experience being artist-leaders by making creative connections. "Taking the Church Out to the World"[51] is one of the transformative activities used in our core Holy Currencies training curriculum. We usually place this exercise toward the last part of the workshop, when we invite church teams to take a ministry they are currently doing out to a location in the neighborhood where people gather. The following are reports from a group of United Methodist churches, which did this exercise in 2014.

1. Mama Bear in the Pub

The Mama Bear ministry of Hyde Park Bethlehem UMC connects needy families with gifts, support, and a party at Christmas time; our church has recently assumed leadership of the program after 30 years of being led by a community member. *(The team was challenged to connect this ministry with a local pub or restaurant.)* Despite the first response of "impossible," we developed a plan for a dine-to-donate program that has great potential to develop relationships and connections to our community.

The plan is to approach a restaurant that would be willing to organize a night when some part of their profits could be donated to our Mama Bear program. We loved the idea of using business cards as a part of the program that could be used to: get a discount at the restaurant (if we work out a deal with the restaurant), identify which patrons came for dine-to-donate, explain that the restaurant was helping to support our program, and most importantly to give phone and e-mail contact for people who are interesting in shopping for/donating presents for the Mama Bear program. Church members could share the cards with friends or give the cards to people as they come in the restaurants. Rather than just leaving "gift tags" on a "giving tree," the e-mail/ phone contact on the cards creates two-way conversations and continuing opportunities to connect with our neighbors, such as a "wrapping" party for those who contributed to wrap Mama Bear gifts, or by creating an (optional, of course) e-mail list for involvement with future dine-to-donate nights or service opportunities.

---

[51]For a full description of "Take the Church Out to the World" exercise, see Eric H. F. Law, *Holy Currencies* (St. Louis: Chalice Press, 2013), 124–25.

Not only will we be able to connect with restaurant staff and neighbors who happen to be dining there, we also will have the possibility of connecting friends with our church through this program (i.e., inviting work friends to dinner and sharing that the profits are going to a ministry in our church).

2. Kid's Outreach—Beyond the Church Walls!

The members of Mt. Sterling UMC decided to move their children's programming outside the walls of the church. This summer, traditional Sunday schools classes will be replaced by such things as "creek stomping," trips to the local museum, and even a meeting at the Dairy Freeze. The purpose is to attract more kids in our community who might be reluctant to sit inside a classroom, but would enjoy hearing about God's love in these different venues.

3. VBS in the Y

Groesbeck UMC is going to take our vacation Bible school (VBS) scheduled for this summer and partner with the YMCA. We will utilize some of our own and some of the YMCA's marketing tools to reach a broader and different community. We will conduct the VBS during the evenings at the YMCA. We then will invite our participants to a worship service on August 10th in the YMCA gym. We will follow that up with a picnic and a pool party in partnership with the YMCA. We will conduct some Grace Margins training in July, with our key 30 to 40 leaders helping us to understand a couple of the key concepts of the training. We will look to apply some of those concepts to the VBS event in August. We will also look to find ways to include parents in the conversation of meeting the needs of children and families in our area. We hope to continue with the YMCA to find additional next steps of connecting with some of these families in new and dynamic ways. We also will attempt to identify viable next steps on the backside of this event. Maybe we can have monthly worship events at the YMCA or community picnics utilizing common ground. We hope to have some teams explore those opportunities down the road. By the way, on August 10th we plan to combine our two services (9:00 and 11:00) and conduct one 10:00 service at the YMCA. We are not sure how all of these details will unfold, but here we go!

4. Partners for Senior Programs

Two churches (Community Church of Riverside UMC and Concord UMC) joined with two nonprofits (Life Enrichment Center and Widows Home of Dayton) to target activities and programs for senior adults. Using Missional Ministry in the Grace Margin as a formational piece to bring the partners together, thirteen persons from the four groups spent 12 hours (in 2 sessions) together. One outcome of the partnership is the CEO of Widows Home working to incorporate the Life Enrichment Center's Catering Service (a program that teaches employable skills to persons seeking work) in the operations of the Widows Home as a sustainable mission. In May, the Widows Home was awarded a $100,000 grant from Dellmar for the partnership's collaboration to leverage their other partners to extend attention to senior activities. Additionally, CareSource, an HMO in Dayton, hearing of the focus on senior activities, has given $10,000 for senior ministries to the poor. One strategy is the creation of a senior council in which seniors are both recipients and deliverers of ministry services. At a luncheon on June 2, Dayton Mayor Nan Whaley met with the partners and encouraged seniors to engage in reading and tutoring the city's 1st and 2nd graders to address improvement in literacy.

How are you an artist-leader? What creative connections can your church community make between the church's resources and the neighborhood community?

82

Entrepreneurial and Sustainable

The board president and the executive director of the Life Enrichment Center (LEC) were giving me a tour. I saw more than 200 people being served hot meals, volunteers putting together bags of groceries to be distributed later, a hair salon, places to get clean clothes and warm showers, and a fitness center complete with personal trainers. And there were rooms for Bible study, sewing, craft, prayers, ESL, GED, and computer classes. Outside, there was a Child Safety Village and a bicycle repair shop. All these are free and staffed by over 60 volunteers, mostly from area churches.

I had been here about eight months ago and was impressed with the comprehensiveness of this ministry. My return visit reaffirmed my initial impressions. But this time, at the end of the tour, I was taken to a room beautifully furnished as a full service café. Eight months ago, it had been an empty room. I recalled that, at that time, we had been exploring how to create an entrepreneurial ministry to move the LEC toward greater sustainability. One of leaders asked me then, "What can we do with this space?" I off-handedly said, "How about a GracEconomics restaurant?" Eight months later, the Findlay Street Café opened.

Its mission, according to the card displayed on each table:

Our aim is to serve quality, affordable food in an atmosphere that promotes personal connections. Café donations support the Life Enrichment Center's free community meals and programs.

Its vision:

The Findlay Street Café strives to be a place of
- Excellence in food and service
- Community, where conversations begin and relationships grow
- Sustenance for patrons, the Life Enrichment Center, and the community

Here are the stories of how it came to be, in question-and-answer format:

Where did the furniture come from?

Someone heard about our idea of the restaurant and decided to donate two professional dip-fryers to the LEC. But our chef said that we wanted to provide healthy food at the café and our menu would most likely not have any fried food items. So, we took the fryers to a professional restaurant equipment store and asked what we could get for them. The owner offered us $3,000. We took the money and bought furniture and material to renovate the place.

How did your chef and volunteers learn to run a professional restaurant?

The chef of One Bistro in Miamisburg allowed our chef to shadow him for three days. He let her help prepare the meals there. He showed us the dos and don'ts in running a restaurant and how to put together a menu. Also, a retired professor of a culinary school volunteered to train our staff to be professional waiters. He did "table talk" to teach us the importance of sitting around a table for a meal. He continues to train our new volunteers.

What is the cost of running the restaurant?

The food is all donated. Everyone involved in running the restaurant is a volunteer. The only paid staff is the chef. The only other expense is the utilities.

How did you get people to come?

We took our menus to the local business offices and let them know that we are open three days a week for lunch. We also take orders by phone and deliver them.

Are you still a not-for-profit organization if you run a restaurant on-site?

We consulted with an accountant on this. When customers finish their lunch, the waiter gives them a bill that says, "This meal is worth $6 at cost. Any additional donation you give will go to supporting the ministries of the Life Enrichment Center. We will give you a donation receipt for that amount."

When did the restaurant become self-sustaining?

As of the end of the second week of operation, the donations from the lunch patrons were more than enough the cover the additional paid staff and utilities to run the café!

I ate there Tuesday and Thursday and was seated at the community table where people are invited to seat with people they may not know especially when they are dining alone. Volunteer waiters, who were professional and friendly, took our orders. The Findlay Street burger was amazing! Through lunch, different individuals joined us and left us and then new patrons were seated with us. Conversations were lively and, of course, we were exploring more new ideas for these kinds of missional and sustainable ministries at the LEC and in Dayton.

During the week, I gave Holy Currencies presentations to the staff, board members, volunteers of the LEC, and leaders from other not-for-profit organizations in Dayton. The discussions were lively and full of potential for making the café even more of a place where people with diverse experiences can connect—building up the currencies of relationship and truth.

The success of the café opens up a floodgate of ideas that can transform the linear-charity model of ministry into circular rejuvenating models that can multiply and self-sustain after the initial "investment." The addition of social businesses can provide training grounds for those served by the ministries, utilizing the currencies that they bring, such as their time and their talents. In other words, in addition to receiving help, they can give back by doing something productive while learning new professional and life skills.

A year later, the café is bringing in $30,000 per year. In addition to the café, they have expanded this ministry to provide fully licensed catering services. The Life Enrichment Center has submitted a grant proposal to create a culinary training program to train people to work in all facets of the restaurant and catering businesses.

I am excited about the future sustainability of the Life Enrichment Center and I intend to continue to resource this already amazing ministry in the future, looking toward launching more sustainable entrepreneurial ministries that will consistently rejuvenate and recirculate resources for the people in Dayton. *The Life Enrichment Center is a faith-based, nonprofit organization providing life-building, life sustaining services for the under-served in the greater Dayton community. Its goal is to optimize physical, spiritual and emotional health: **because everyone has value.***

83

Holy Currency Mission Statement

Having a missional idea is one thing; making it real takes time and intentionality. We begin by creating a mission statement based on the idea. Very often, a mission statement can be too long, unfocused, and static. A holy currency mission statement captures the dynamic exchanges of two or more currencies. Here is the step-by-step process:

1. What is the product or service this ministry provides? (The product or service can be any of the currencies: time, place, gracious leadership, relationship, truth, wellness, and money.)
2. Who are your clients/guests?
3. What are the benefits/blessings that this ministry cultivates? In other words, what blessings do the product/service plus the client/guest exchange into? (Again, blessings can be any of the currencies: time, place, gracious leadership, relationship, truth, wellness, and money.)
4. Create a mission statement based on your answers to the above questions by combining the following two simple sentences:
    a. We provide *[product or service]* for *[customer/client/guest]*.
    b. We help *[customers/client/guest]* "do"/"achieve"/"other verb" *[primary benefit/blessing]*.

Example:

The Kaleidoscope Institute provides resources to equip church leaders to create sustainable churches and communities.

Try writing a mission statement for an existing or new ministry using this process. Be sure to capture the dynamic flow of more than one blessing. For example, "We provide food for the hungry," is a static statement because it only utilizes one exchange. However, "We provide food, a place, and a community network for people to discern a sustainable future," is a dynamic mission statement that names exchanges of the currencies of wellness, place, and relationship.

84

The Evergreen Way

The Evergreen Baptist Association gathered at Japanese Baptist Church in Seattle on February 22, 2003, for a historic meeting to adopt by-laws. These by-laws are unique for an American Baptist Region. They are historic on two counts:

- The organizational structure of the region is in the form of ethnic caucuses, and
- Decision-making is by consensus.

It all began with a debate in the American Baptist Churches of the Northwest (ABC/NW). A by-law proposal that would have expelled congregations that were in the Association of Welcoming and Affirming Baptists[52] failed by the slimmest of margins because it did not have the supermajority required at the May 2000 Biennial Convention of ABC/NW. Another resolution that did pass stated:

> With deep regret, we acknowledge that a reorganization of the Region is necessary, and call for a regional process, including the proposed self-study, to determine the configuration of the new regional structure, to be determined on or before May 2002 with an interim report to the churches in May 2001.[53]

After this decision, ABC/NW decided to form a new region with churches in the Seattle area being the nucleus. Through the process of self-study, as well as time spent listening to the dreams, vision, passions, and concerns of the constituencies, this group selected a new name: "Evergreen." The Rev. Marcia Patton became the first Executive Minister. She came to one of the first Kaleidoscope Training Institutes in 2005. Having read some of my books—in particular, *The Wolf Shall Dwell with the Lamb*—she was looking for ways to enhance the already-formed structure and decision-making process of Evergreen. In the incubation of this new organization, the leadership insisted that the currency of truth was what had to flow in, through, and out of this organization. Marcia wrote in the "historic blog" at the Evergreen website:[54]

> Evergreen is blessed as an organization, especially blessed as an American Baptist Region because of our beginnings. We were born

---

[52]See awab.org/history.html.
[53]See http://www.evergreen-abc.org/history.html.
[54]The following paragraphs are excerpts from the historic blog of Evergreen Association at http://www.evergreen-abc.org/blogs.html.

out of the controversy surrounding acceptance of gay/lesbian/transgendered/bisexual peoples in American Baptist life... There was a caveat that any church in SBU (Seattle Baptist Union) could opt out of the new region and any church in the greater ABC Northwest could opt into the new region... This was a gift of a clean slate, an empty place, in which to build something new. This gift allowed us to begin with renewing relationships and work slowly toward organization...

We had also adopted by-laws that called for caucus groups to be our structure. This is instead of some kind of geographical representative structure. But it guaranteed voice and understanding to people who otherwise did not feel that they have voice and understanding. We started by making sure that we began a rotation of the chair by the African-American caucus group, not the Euro-American caucus group. Real genius was experienced when we put our consensus decision-making and our caucus structure together. When we are even in mid-size groups (our Association Board for instance), consensus is gained in caucus groups and brought back to the group as whole... This works particularly well for the caucuses of color. In the relative safety of their caucus groups they can say and figure out things in ways better for them than they ever could working in the group as a whole.

The benefits of the caucus system were not known early on. One of the best unintended consequences is that we don't have a nomination committee for Evergreen. Each caucus acts as it needs to put forth nominations. Talk about sharing of power. Without a nomination committee in Evergreen, power is more dispersed and shared. The caucus system allows each caucus to handle nominations in its own way. In fact, each caucus is organized in its own way!

The quorum, across Evergreen, is that at least one person from each caucus must be present in order for us to do business. For all people groups, this says, if we don't show up, it means that the organization cannot go forward. The rules say we can only get along with everyone present! That is a real shift for people of color; it means ownership in a way that is not usual—in American Baptist circles anyway.

In addition, our caucuses help us reach consensus. Early on in our life, we learned that consensus-building as a whole group beyond the Executive Committee (total 7 people) was almost impossible. The caucuses allowed us immediate smaller groups!... I'm convinced at times conversations happen that just would not happen if the group [caucus] were ethnically mixed... Does it mean that sometimes decisions must be slowed down? Yes! So far that hasn't been a bad thing. It has helped us all come to more reasoned decisions and decision-making.

Sharing the Evergreen way is simple and complex. Our consensus and caucus work makes us unique in a lot of cultures. Our determination to work toward making every voice count means we are doing things differently. Our business and our play/work times have a different flavor and sense than whatever was before. We don't want to say in any way that we have arrived. But we are on a collective journey that is interesting and fun and has the sense of God's blessings.

The Mission of Evergreen Association:

Being a culturally diverse people who are one in Christ and who value the liberties of our American Baptist heritage, the Evergreen Baptist Association will:

- Build bridges between communities;
- Provide resources to equip member churches to share Christ and teach God's word;
- Translate our unity to the world.

Our Purpose:

Evergreen churches build bridges that carry the message of who we are and accept the message of who others are. Those bridges open the door for creation of relationships. Relationships begin through participation in Evergreen that leads to an increased number of people being involved, and intentional intergenerational connections. Those relationships result in sensitivity to our cultural differences, so that more people now live and tell the Evergreen story.

85

Holy Currency Ministry-Business Plan

Incubating a missional and sustainable ministry requires the planners to work through the cycle of blessings, ensuring each of the currencies will flow and rejuvenate each other in the new ministry. The biggest mistake is for planners to move too quickly without making sure that all the currencies are in place. The incubation process therefore can take some time. For example, if in the exploration of the currency of internal and external relationships, the planners discover that they don't have a strong external network, they will need to take some time to develop these relationships before launch. If the planners realize that they don't know the truth about the real needs and concerns of the people in the community, they will need to create opportunities to listen for the truth before they make any concrete plans. At the end of the exploration, create a ministry plan that will incorporate all the currencies using the following outline:

a. Name the wellness (physical, social, ecological, economical, and/or spiritual) you are fostering in this new ministry.
b. Name the truth that you are seeking through this ministry or the truth to which this ministry responds.
c. Construct a relational network (internal and external) that supports this ministry.
d. Establish a place and time in which this ministry will take place.
e. Name or develop the "product" or "by-product" for which people with financial resources would be willing to pay.
f. Clarify the expectation of the clients/guests to pay back using the currencies they have.
g. Create a wellness plan for people involved (both workers and clients/guests).
h. Develop leadership training processes to empower people for this ministry (both workers and clients/guests).
i. Find initial investors to give money, time, and talent to launch this ministry.
j. Formulate a plan for ongoing financial sustainability.
k. Project a timeframe when this ministry will be self-sustaining.

86

Life Skillz Circle

In 2012, two members of First Presbyterian Church in San Bernardino, California, went to a Presbytery-sponsored Holy Currencies workshop. While we were exploring the currencies of truth and wellness, one of them shared that the high school next door to their church had only a 27 percent graduation rate. The truth of unwellness drove us to explore what the church might do to foster wellness for the young people in their community. One of the ideas that caught a lot of energy was to train caring adult volunteers from the church to meet with tenth graders once a week in order to provide more stability and a support network that could help them develop life skills. We were calling this idea Life Skillz Circle. They brought the idea back to their church and the leadership agreed to invest some money, from a recent inheritance, to commission the Kaleidoscope Institute to assist them in this effort. So I reentered the conversation as their consultant, moving them through an incubation period before launch.

At the first meeting, the planning group was talking with enthusiasm about starting this program to invite the young people to come to the church after school. They had the idea, they had the money, they were eager to help, and they were ready to go! As I guided them in exploring each currency of the cycle of blessings, they realized that they didn't have strong relationships with the school—teachers, students, parents, principal, or counselors. As their consultant, I challenged them to develop their currency of relationship with the school for a period of six months.

So the pastor and a group of lay leaders made an appointment to see the principal of the school. They told her that they were members of this community and they were concerned about the low graduation rate at the school. They were not there to judge nor to proselytize, but to explore ways that they could help. To their surprise, the principal enthusiastically shared with them a list of things that they could do. During the following six months in 2013, members of the church wrote a thousand notes of encouragement and sent a carload of snacks to the students while they were taking the state test; they hosted an end-of-season celebration at the church for two sports teams; they patronized the school's bakery and flower shop, and some of them volunteered to assist in the Safety Ambassador program. The principal attended their planning meetings regularly and, when she could not attend, she would send a school counselor in her place.

A year after the initial idea of the Life Skillz Circle was named, the currency of relationship was now well-developed. Through these relationships, church members discovered the truth that they needed to know in order to launch this ministry. Initially, they thought that the students would come to the church after school for their weekly gatherings. After listening to the principal, the counselors, the teachers, and students they had gotten to know, they determined that the best time was Monday morning at 8 a.m., and the best place to meet was one of the classrooms. The currency of truth exchanged into a relocation of their currency of time and place. And, of course, food would be a major factor to keep the students coming.

In the fall of 2013, they were planning to launch the first Life Skillz Circle in January. At the meeting, the principal said she wanted to make sure this first circle would be a success; she and the counselor would personally invite the first group of tenth graders to participate in this pilot group. The currency of relationship was paying off.

There were apprehensions, however, among the church members about whether they were ready to do this. As one of the empty nesters said, "I have time, but what do I have to offer these students? What if the answer is nothing but my 'mom-ness'? In holy currency terminology, they were in need of developing their currency of gracious leadership. While they were building relationships with the school, I worked with a group of church members and teachers and developed a 12-week curriculum incorporating the basic gracious leadership skills taught by the Kaleidoscope Institute. In the late fall of 2013, I facilitated a gracious leadership training session for caring adults who could serve as group leaders using the Life Skillz Circle curriculum.

The first week of 2014, these volunteers stood in room B109, armed with worksheets, sign-in sheets, and get-to-know-you surveys, wondering if any students would come. Who would eat all this breakfast food? Slowly, the students arrived, looking anxious and not entirely sure why they were there. One of the volunteers wrote in a report of that first session:

> In that first hour, one of them tells us his parents are separating, and he is torn: which house should he choose? And we know we are in the right place. You would love these kids: the quiet, caring 4.0 GPA football player and member of the track team; the sweet and funny AVID student and her best friend who loves Zombie movies and has a "sixth sense" about things; the sophomore class president who loves European history and is a self-proclaimed nerd; and the football quarterback who is determined to succeed despite immeasurable odds. They are smart, funny, and surprisingly comfortable with us.
>
> [The Life Skillz] curriculum gave us confidence to engage in this process and many of the elements have provided some great discussions… At times I have worried about what I will say or do at a given meeting, but a turning point for me was hearing one of

them say, "I just like talking." Maybe all they are asking is to be seen and to be heard... just like the rest of us.

At the end of the spring semester, the students expressed the need to continue meeting. A volunteer recalled, "One student shared that if we were to stop this, he would feel lost. Our hope is to be there when he graduates in 2016." They met a few more times at church members' homes and they also took two students on a field trip to the University of Redlands, where college students shared their college experiences and connected with them as only young people could.

By the summer of 2014, the good people of First Presbyterian Church had become a fixture at San Bernardino High School. They brought leftovers from breakfast every Monday to the front office and had hosted Mr. Cardinal[55] mock interviews, getting to know more amazing students. The school asked the church to expand the Life Skillz Circle, incorporating it into a new leadership curriculum, taking on a group of freshman in the fall.

At the start of the school year, the students from the first circle now served as ambassadors for the Life Skillz Circle by talking to the freshmen encouraging them to join a new circle. One of the church volunteers, who went with four of them to two classes, reported, "I was overwhelmed by their insight into what this group is becoming and what it means to them. One student said it had become his other family and they all talked about the friendship, trust, and enjoyment they find with this group. As always, I feel blessed to have the opportunity to work with these kids. They fill my heart."

As of the fall of 2014, there are two Life Skillz Circles at San Bernardino High School—one with the original group plus their friends, and the other with a group of freshmen. And the cycle of blessings continues.

> The Lord God has given me
>   the tongue of a teacher,
> that I may know how to sustain
>   the weary with a word.
> Morning by morning he wakens—
>   wakens my ear
>   to listen as those who are taught.
>   (Isaiah 50:4–5)

---

[55]Mr. Cardinal City is a pageant for young men during their junior year to compete for the honor of being Mr. Cardinal as a senior at San Bernadino High School. The competition is based on grades, community service, appearance in formal wear and sportswear, and interviews.

87

Holy Currency Job Description

The holy currencies/cycle of blessings is a way of life. It affects everything we think and do. It shapes how we plan our day. It conditions our way of discerning our ministries, our stewardship, our mission statements, and our ministry plans. It shapes every job we take on. Here is a process for writing a volunteer job description incorporating the cycle of blessings. Notice how this job description, through the exploration of the wellness currency and gracious leadership, takes care of one of the biggest complaints from organizations that employ volunteers: the same people doing the same jobs again and again, while at the same time, complaining that nobody else is willing to help, and feeling overworked and burnt out. Try to write a volunteer job description using the following outline for every volunteer you have in your organization. If you are a volunteer yourself and you don't have a job description, try writing one using the following template. Working through this job description will not only create a more sustainable volunteer network but also a more sustainable ministry.

Holy Currency Volunteer Job Description

Position Title: A specific, descriptive title provides the volunteer with a sense of identity and ensures that salaried staff and other volunteers understand this particular role.

Purpose of the Position: Describe how the volunteer's work contributes to the mission of the ministry.

Responsibilities: Identify the position's specific responsibilities and duties.

Qualifications: These may include gifts, personal characteristics, skills, abilities, education, and/or experience required.

(Currency of Place)

Ministry Location: Where will the individual be working? Can the work be done at home or only on site, or at a particular site?

(Currency of Time)

Time Commitment: Include length of service, hours per week, hours per day. Include any special requirements such as weekend work.

(Currency of Wellness)

Wellness Plan: Describe the sabbatical plan for this position—for example, for every 10 months of work, the volunteer will take two months off. For every three years in the same position, the volunteer will take a year off. Include other wellness provisions to foster physical, spiritual, and relational wellness for the volunteer.

(Currency of Gracious Leadership)

Training: List the training that the volunteer will receive. Include general gracious leadership training that all positions receive, plus any position-specific training for this assignment. Include the volunteer's responsibility to train others to do the job while he/she takes a sabbatical.

(Currency of Relationship)

Network: Describe the relationship networks of which the volunteer will be part. Include to whom he/she will be accountable—both paid staff and other volunteers, committee, work group, taskforce, support group, spiritual director, or worship community.

(Currency of Money)

Finance: The budget for this ministry that the volunteer will have access to. Reimbursement process for expenses.

(Currency of Truth)

Ministry Review: Describe the process by which the volunteer will be evaluated. How often will this occur, and who will be involved in the process? This is also the time for the volunteer to share his/her experiences, speaking the truth, so that the ministry can be continuously improved.

Benefits: What will the volunteer gain by taking this position? What is the currency exchange? Include leadership skills; stronger relationship network; discernment of the truth about self, others, and the world; development of wellness.

88

Pledge Card for the Currency of Gracious Leadership

Gracious leadership is the key to mobilizing the cycle of blessings. Specifically, gracious leaders have the ability to create a gracious environment in which people of diverse backgrounds and experiences can build trusting relationships and speak truth to each other in love. Gracious leaders also assist the church and the community in truthful dialogue on concerns and issues that they face while moving the community toward greater wellness. In other words, gracious leadership ensures that the church's ministries are relational and missional.

On this final pledge card, we invite church members to make a commitment—first, in offering the leadership skills they already have for ministries inside and outside the church. Then, we invite church members to commit to developing their currency of gracious leadership. The easiest way to make this happen is for the church to provide periodic gracious leadership training programs. Of course, church members can also research what is available outside the geographical area, and make a commitment to pay for and travel to the gracious leadership training programs of their choice.

Two additional pieces are embedded in this pledge card. Church members are invited to mentor new gracious leaders in the church for specific ministries. For example, someone who has been functioning as a relational greeter may pledge to train another to do the same. Church members are also invited to make a commitment to mentor leaders outside the church. For example, a church member may volunteer to be an adult mentor for a local school safety ambassador program.

Make a commitment today using this pledge card. Find an Accountable Person to sign it and submit it to your church. Make this pledge card an opportunity for dialogue and teaching about the importance of the currency of gracious leadership.

Pledge Card for the Currency of Gracious Leadership

- I commit to offering my ability to _____ (name of leadership skills) in support of _____ (name of existing or new ministry in my church or community).
- I commit to participating in _____ (name of leadership training programs) in order to become a more gracious leader in my church and/or the community.
- I commit to mentoring and/or training _____ new leaders in my church to do/be _____.
- I commit to mentoring and/or training _____ leaders in the community to do/be _____.

My name: _____ My accountable person: _____

_____   _____
      signature   signature

Date: _____

89

A Holy Currencies Picture

As more church leaders participate in the Holy Currencies training through the Kaleidoscope Institute, we are witnessing more practical applications of our model, tools, and concepts. Below is one from the St. James's Episcopal Church in Cambridge, Massachusetts. The rector, the Rev. Holly Lyman Antolini, came to one of our earliest Holy Currencies trainings. As part of a stewardship campaign, she created the following graphic incorporating the ministries of St James's Church and the six currencies:[56]

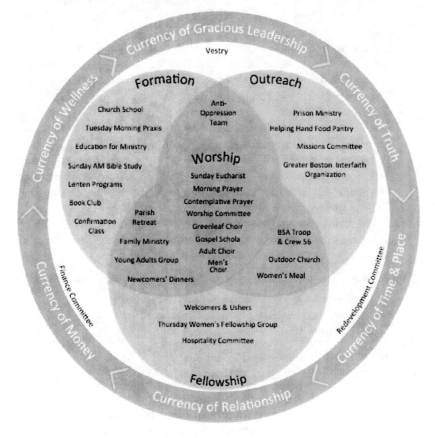

---

[56]Discover more about the stewardship process of St. James's Episcopal Church at http://www.stjames-cambridge.org/.

The following is Part Two of the stewardship packet St. James's sent out to its members. Part One is for pledging of the currency of money. Shown here is the linear version of the graphic, inviting church members to consider making commitments to maintain, support, and develop all six holy currencies:

Increasing our Holy Currencies to Sustain God's Mission

(Circle any of the following that interest you!)

- **Currency of Gracious Leadership:** Nominating Committee, Vestry, Alewife Deanery Representative, Diocesan Convention representative, Episcopal City Mission Liaison, Personnel Committee, Church School teachers
- **Currency of Relationship:** 20's & 30's Group, Nursery Families, Church School Families, GBLTQ group, Women's Meal, Welcomer Ministry, Ushers, Bible Study, PRAXIS *lectio divina* group, Book Group, Adult Formation Committee
- **Currency of Truth:** Prison Ministry, Greater Boston Interfaith Organization, Helping Hand Food Pantry, Women's Meal, Missions Committee, Outdoor Church, Anti-Oppression Team
- **Currency of Wellness:** Hospitality Committee, St. James's Choir, Men's Choir, Worship Committee, Readers/Intercessors, Chalicers Acolytes, Eucharistic Visitors, Healing Prayers E-List
- **Currency of Time & Place:** Property Committee, Altar Guild, Redevelopment Committee
- **Currency of Money:** Finance Committee, Investment Committee, Revenue Enhancement Task Force, Audit Committee, Currency of Money Pledge Campaign Committee

Please check here if you want someone to contact you about a ministry.

___I want someone to contact me about participating in one of the ministries that increase our Holy Currencies or about something I feel called to start.

Phone number (I prefer a call) _____
E-mail (I prefer an e-mail)_____

If you were to draw a diagram of your church's ministry incorporating the cycle of blessings, what would it look like? In what ways can you invite church members to make commitments to all the currencies of the cycle of blessings?

90

Truth or Trick or Treat

"Even when the economy is shuffling along like a zombie, Americans aren't scared to spend big bucks on Halloween," a newscaster said on the radio. "A recent survey reports that the average person will spend $72.32 on Halloween—or about $6.8 billion nationwide. Out of the average total, we're buying at least $20 worth of candy alone. And to make sure our pets get the most of the holiday, we're shelling out $310 million on pet costumes."[57] The results of the survey administered by the National Retail Federation got airtime on every news station, both TV and radio, in 2011.[58] Overall, Halloween had beaten out Thanksgiving, the Fourth of July, and Easter, and was only outdone by Christmas when it came to total spending.

All the news reports gave the impression that this "scary" spending was good for the economy, but it probably wouldn't help its long-term recovery. While I appreciated other news reports on tips to keep children safe and ways to help them stay healthy in the midst of tempting sweets, I couldn't help but notice that the currency of money had crept in as the only measuring rod of success of this holiday.

I did a little research on the tradition of "trick or treat" and found that the practice of dressing up in costumes and begging door to door for treats on holidays dated back to the Middle Ages and included Christmas wassailing. Trick-or-treating resembled the late medieval practice of souling, when poor folk would go door to door on Hallowmas (November 1), receiving food and money in return for prayers for the dead on All Souls Day (November 2).

Yes, the tradition of trick or treat was partly about money, but it was not about how much people spent to support the economy. It was about poor people in need and rich people who could give, and the exchanges were prayers and songs. Perhaps Halloween is supposed to remind us of the uneven distribution of resources in our communities and that on this one night, at least, we would acknowledge it, or there would be unfortunate consequences (such as mischief and tricks).

The Occupy Movement that started on Wall Street was unintentionally following the original spirit of Halloween. The protesters were knocking on the doors of corporations insisting that they acknowledge the financial injustices that the financial corporations had instigated. (This was the treat

---

[57]See http://consumerist.com/2011/10/31/americans-spend-about-68-billion-total-on-halloween/.

[58] For the latest survey result on spending on Halloween, see https://nrf.com/resources/halloween-headquarters.

that the protesters demanded.) As long as the financial institutions and the political players ignored them, they would continue to occupy strategic places, legally and illegally. (This was the trick.) The difference between this movement and Halloween was that they were not looking for just one night of acknowledgment and a little handout in exchange for appeasement. They were building an international relationship network; they were helping each other to continue speaking the truth, in spite of the aggressive reactions of the system—arrests, tear gas, confiscation of generators and heaters as winter approached. They were using other currencies such as relationship and truth to move communities toward financial, social, and spiritual wellness. The external expressions of the Occupy Movement might have faded away, but the spirit of what it started, hopefully, will continue.

Perhaps during the week when we celebrate Halloween, All Soul's Day, and All Saints' Day—and all future holidays, for that matter—we can decide not to worship money. Instead, we can reframe our measure of success using other currencies such as truth, wellness, relationship, and leadership.

Reframe a Holiday

Invite members of your community to come together to explore the following question:

> What would the celebration of Halloween be like if we decided to measure our success using the following currencies:
>
> 1. Leadership, 2. Relationship, 3. Truth, 4. Wellness

1. Form four small groups and give each group one of the above "currencies"—leadership, relationship, truth, or wellness. Invite each group to explore new rituals, events, and processes that would help participants of the celebration to develop this currency. (Here are some examples: For leadership, create costumes of important leaders for children to wear in your community; engage the children in an exploration of what made them great leaders. For relationship, instead of just handing out candy, invite the children/parents in your house and have a getting-to-know-each-other activity. For wellness, offer a wellness and safety workshop for parents and children before they go out trick-or-treating.)
2. Invite each group to report.
3. As a large group select four or five action items to be implemented for next year's Halloween.

(You can use this process to assist your community in exploring how to refocus the upcoming holidays such as Thanksgiving and Christmas— to achieve relationship truth leadership and wellness.)

91

A Holy Currency Thanksgiving

My Hebrew Scripture professor, Harvey Guthrie, once said in his class on the Psalms, "Thanksgiving is about remembering." In the biblical tradition, to give thanks to God is to remember what God has done for us. The people of Israel gave thanks by remembering how God had delivered them from the oppression of the Egyptians, and from slavery to freedom through the Exodus experience. In remembering this event, they gave thanks to God by offering a sacrifice. The sacrifice of an animal was a sign, an action that symbolized this remembrance. And, then, by remembering and taking a symbolic action, we renew our vows to be faithful to God.

> Offer to God a sacrifice of thanksgiving
> and pay your vows to the Most high. (Psalm 50:14)

In Psalm 50, the psalmist sang about how God did not want our sacrifice as a hollow gesture with no meaning and leading to little actions (i.e., no holy currency exchanges.) To the psalmist, the best sacrifice we can offer is to give thanks. This thanksgiving should move us to renewing and keeping our vows—our promises—to God.

As we remember the blessings we have received, and as we give thanks, we must renew our promise to sustain each other and the earth so that the blessings will continue to flow. Here is a holy currency approach to celebrating Thanksgiving. You can do this on your own or with a group.

1. **Recall an event:**
   a. Review this past year and recall an event of blessing or transformation for you.
   b. Write down the sequence of events leading to this blessing or transformation.
   c. Name the persons or groups who facilitated this transformation. Describe their actions.

2. **Symbolic Action:**
   a. Create a symbolic action that can help you remember this event. This symbolic action may or may not involve the people who facilitated your transformation. For example, the symbolic action can be writing a thank-you card to a person affirming the blessings that this person has been for you. Other symbolic actions may include inviting another to a meal, offering a gift,

creating a photo album, creating a video, or making a public announcement.

3. Renew a Promise:

    a. As part of your symbolic action, offer or renew a promise that you will carry out for the persons or community involved. A promise might be: "I will volunteer at the homeless shelter for this coming year," or, "I will spend 15 minutes a day in prayer," or, "I will visit with a person at least once a month."

Thanksgiving, as a holiday, is a time to gather family and friends to remember and give thanks. A holy currency Thanksgiving moves us to continue the flow of blessings. We do this by taking the gifts for which we are thankful and exchanging them for that which is holy—expanding the currencies of relationship, truth, and wellness.

92

Offer to God a Sacrifice

Offer to God a Sacrifice

Canon

Of-fer to God a sac-ri-fice,_____ a sac-ri - fice of thanks-

giv-ing,_____ and make good your vows to the Most High,_____ and

make good your vows to the Most High._____

For a small group of altos and basses, in unison

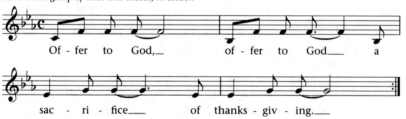

Of - fer to God,__ of - fer to God___ a

sac - ri - fice_____ of thanks - giv - ing.__

Accompaniment

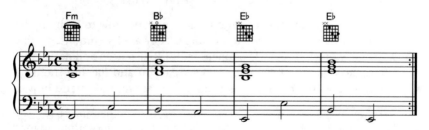

93

Straight Path to the Truth

Since 2008, the U.S. government has come up with one solution after another to fix the economy, but none seem to work very well. The nation's economy seems so complicated that few people can really figure out what is going on. Did anyone really comprehend how bailing out the banks actually helped people to recover their livelihood? Does anyone remember that, in 2011, Congress set up the so-called "Super Committee" to decide what to cut, in order to reduce the nation's deficit? If you remember, were you as confused as I was that the Super Committee came up with nothing? My tax dollars were spent on 12 well-fed politicians in a room for over two months, coming up with nothing!

Around Thanksgiving weekend, the national media are always buzzing with statistics on consumer spending on Thanksgiving Day, Black Friday, and Cyber Monday. Over the Thanksgiving weekend of 2014, people in the U.S. spent more than $50 billion shopping. This was good news, according to Henry Hazlitt, author of *Economics in One Lesson,* because consumer spending accounts for about 70 percent of the nation's economy.[59] I have heard this line about the 70 percent of the economy many times—on radio, TV, and in print media—but what does it really mean? The best I could decipher from it is that when people like you and me spend our money to buy stuff, our economy will recover.

"The voice of one crying out in the wilderness:
'Prepare the way of the Lord,
    make his paths straight.
Every valley shall be filled,
    and every mountain and hill shall be made low,
and the crooked shall be made straight,
    and the rough ways made smooth;
and all flesh shall see the salvation of God.'" (Luke 3:4–6)

These things we are told about our economy and how to fix it are like crooked roads that seem to lead to nowhere. They are like mountains that block the view of what really is happening. It is like a deep and dark valley has been placed between everyday people like you and me and the truth that we can't possibly recognize as reality. If we are to understand how to

---

[59]I found this information in an article, "The Importance of Consumer Spending," by Osmond Vitez at the website: http://smallbusiness.chron.com/importance-consumer-spending-3882.html.

revitalize our economy, we need some straight paths to the truth.

Hector Delgadillo, CEO of Turbo Coil, bought a whole page of the October 20, 2011, issue of *The Pasadena Weekly* to publish an open letter to President Barack Obama and members of Congress. In this letter, he wrote:

> I used to buy Ralph Lauren suits, shirts and pants. They used to be made in the U.S.A. I paid top dollar. Then they moved their production to China. Funny thing though, the prices stayed the same or even increased. Why? Even when the manufacturing costs were lower? More money goes into Mr. Ralph Lauren's pocket. And the lower costs are due to slave labor that is used to build these and other leading consumer brands: Nike, Puma, Calvin Klein, New Balance, Eileen Fisher, Apple, Motorola, J. Crew, Gap, and Zara.

Apparently, the people who storm the malls looking for bargains are not the ones responsible for the recovery of our economy after all. Their spending, however large, will probably not revitalize our economy in the long run. Take a look at the labels of the things people buy on Black Friday or Cyber Monday. When we spend more than $50 billion over the Thanksgiving weekend, whose economy are we revitalizing? Not the United States. The clothes I am wearing right now are made in the Dominican Republic, Columbia, and China. In fact, everything I have on was made somewhere other than the U.S.

The English words "economy" and "economics" can be traced back to the Greek words οἰκονόμος (pronounced oy-kon-om'-os), i.e., "one who manages a household," a composite word derived from οἶκος (pronounce oy'-kos meaning "house") and νέμω (pronounced ne-mō meaning "manage; distribute").[60] When I manage my household, I track where my money comes from, and where it goes. If we are to be good managers of our common household—our nation—we need to take a look at where the money might come from first. The government doesn't have it; the tax money we pay does not seem to be enough to cover our spending and that's why we have a huge deficit. The banks have money, but are not lending it out readily to the good people who need it. The 99 percent, as the Occupy Wall Street movement once called us, doesn't have the money either; that's why we stay up all night after Thanksgiving to get to the stores for that bargain—we need to save a few dollars. Yet the spotlight is constantly on us, watching how we spend our money—and we are continuously being urged to "save the economy."

Here is a straight path to the truth: the rich have the money; that's why they are called rich. So why don't we put the spotlight on the rich and watch how they spend their money? Better yet, we can challenge them to

---

[60]I found these origins and definitions in an article compiled by Benedict Afful Jr. at http://wikieducator.org/images/b/bc/Fundamental_concepts_of_an_economynew.pdf.

spend in ways that will actually boost our economy. They are the ones who can put money back in circulation so that resources can flow through the wider system, rejuvenating more people and communities. Here are some suggestions for the rich:

1. Buy U.S.-made products even when they cost more. Why? Because you can afford it.
2. Create local jobs in your own communities. According to Wikipedia, there were approximately 7.1 million people living in the United States who were classified as millionaires in 2013.[61] If every millionaire in the U.S. took a small fraction of his or her income and created two jobs locally, there would be 14 million new local jobs. How is that for helping the recovery of our economy? If you need help in creating jobs, just look around your neighborhood, town, or city; see what needs to be done for the benefit of the community; and pay people to do it. It is that simple.
3. Use your influence to keep jobs in the U.S., even though it means you may make a little less money. You will feel much better knowing that you are providing good salaries and health benefit for fellow citizens.
4. Use your influence to make sure that the U.S.-made products are of high quality and that they are beneficial to the environment and to those who will buy them. Have pride in what we make.

---

[61]See http://en.wikipedia.org/wiki/Millionaire.

94

Leveling the Playing Field

"Approximately 8-in-10 (79%) of Americans believe the gap between the rich and the poor has gotten larger over the past 20 years," a November 2011 Public Religion Research Institute Survey revealed.[62] However, Americans were more divided about the impact of this perceived rise in inequality on the idea of the American Dream. Two-thirds (67%) said the government should do more to reduce the gap between the rich and the poor. When the results were broken down by political party, there was a striking 40-point gap between Republicans and Democrats on this question; more than 8-in-10 (83%) Democrats agreed that the government should do more to reduce the gap between the rich and the poor, compared to only 43% of Republicans. Nearly 7-in-10 (68%) of Americans said that in order to reduce the national deficit, it is fair to ask wealthier Americans to pay a greater percentage in taxes than the middle class or those less well-off.[63]

I don't imagine these numbers have changed much since 2011. Given the state of Congress, I am not surprise that there are seemingly irreconcilable differences of opinion on whether the government should get involved in reducing the gap between the rich and the poor.

Here are some biblical texts for the Advent season that might help us think through this.

> The spirit of the Lord GOD is upon me,
>   because the LORD has anointed me;
> he has sent me to bring good news to the oppressed,
>   to bind up the brokenhearted,
> to proclaim liberty to the captives,
>   and release to the prisoners;
> to proclaim the year of the LORD's favor,. . . (Isaiah 61:1–2a)

> May those who sow in tears
>   reap with songs of joy.

> Those who go out weeping, bearing the seed for sowing,
> shall come home with shouts of joy, carrying their sheaves.
> (Psalm 126:6–7)

> [God] has scattered the proud in the thoughts of their hearts.

---

[62]See http://publicreligion.org/research/2011/11/november-2011-rns/#.VTuveWTBzGc.

[63]Ibid.

He has brought down the powerful from their thrones,
 and lifted up the lowly;
he has filled the hungry with good things,
 and sent the rich away empty. (Luke 1:51–53)

These texts and many others in the Hebrew and Christian Scriptures reveal a pattern of God's attitude toward the poor and the rich, the powerless and the powerful. The text from Luke, traditionally called the <u>Magnificat</u> or the Song of Mary, gives us the dynamic divine action of lifting up the lowly while casting down the mighty.

Whether the government should be involved in reducing the gap between the rich and poor, you can decide. Not only that, but you can help determine the outcome by using your political influence through your vote and by other means. It is significant that two-thirds of Americans believe the government should be more involved. In the last few years, there have been voices crying out in the wilderness, such as the Occupy Movement, calling for the leveling of the economic playing field. For people of faith who read and follow the Hebrew and Christian Scriptures, we are called to follow God's patterns, and one of these patterns is to act in ways that will level the economic and political playing field by lifting up the poor and challenging the rich to give.

Rich and Poor

Gather your community for a conversation about being rich and poor.

Invite participants to identify whether they consider themselves:
- rich
- poor
- not sure

Invite them to form three groups according how they identify themselves and consider the following questions:
- What criteria did you use to determine whether you are rich or poor or not sure?
- What feelings did this exercise conjure up for you?
- What responsibilities do you have as a person with this economic identity?

Invite each group to report on the three questions, beginning with the group that identifies itself as "poor," and then "not sure" and finally "rich."

Conclude by inviting each person to complete the sentences:
- I notice...
- I wonder...

95

Sun of Righteousness
(An Advent Blessing)

May the sun of righteousness
Shine upon, shine upon you.
May the sun scatter the darkness
Scatter the darkness
Scatter the darkness
From before your path.
May the sun of grace and truth
Shine upon, shine upon you.
May the sun warm you with justice
Warm you with justice
Warm you with justice
As you walk your path.
May the blessing of God
The Creator, the Redeemer and the Sustainer
Be among you
Be among you
And remain with you always,
Amen.

Sun of Righteousness

96

Beware, Keep Alert

"It was a year of grand juries and smashed windows, of tear gas and video evidence, and of boisterous demands for police reform in Los Angeles, New York, Oakland and Ferguson, Mo., as crowds cried, 'Black lives matter,'" begins a *Los Angeles Times* article by Matt Pearce published on December 31, 2014.

It was the year in which Eric Garner, a black Staten Island man suspected of selling untaxed cigarettes, died after an altercation with police; the officer accused of putting him in an unauthorized chokehold was not indicted. Ohio police were similarly absolved after fatally shooting John Crawford III in a Wal-Mart where he picked up a BB gun and walked around the store while talking on the phone with his girlfriend. Elsewhere in Ohio, a Cleveland police officer fatally shot a 12-year-old boy, Tamir Rice, who was playing with a toy gun in a neighborhood park—a death the state medical examiner ruled a homicide.

In city after city, 2014 became a year in which the nation's lingering racial fissures burst from the strain of a fundamental disagreement over the nature and purpose of policing, especially in African American communities.

A CBS news report compared protests in New York City and Ferguson, after grand juries in both locations decided not to indict the officers, Daniel Pantaleo and Darren Wilson, involved in the shootings of Eric Garner and Michael Brown. The comparison pointed out that, in New York, the police force was more prepared to handle the crowd, and the protesters were more orderly and nonviolent. But the praises of preparedness disappeared not long after that, when two police officers were killed in their patrol car in Brooklyn, solely because of the uniforms they wore. At the funeral, hundreds of N.Y.P.D. officers turned their backs on the mayor, Bill de Blasio, increasing the tension between the mayor's office, the police department, and the African American communities.

Just how ready are we to deal with such events? For many from historically oppressed communities, our reaction might be, "Here we go again; we know this pattern of police brutality has been going for a long time and the justice system doesn't care; when is it ever going to change?" Others might be surprised by the angry reactions: "What is all this about? The police and the grand juries are just doing their jobs." Yet no one can deny the tension, confrontation, polarization, and, in Ferguson, destruction that these events caused.

If this is a pattern, why are we continually surprised when it replays itself? I recall the Los Angeles Riots of 1992—the violent reactions to the acquittal of the five police officers who were caught on videotape beating Rodney King. We were surprised then, and why are we still surprised now? My answer: we were not prepared and we did not do anything afterward to prepare ourselves, our communities, our justice system, or our law enforcement to be ready. So, we are surprised when it happens again.

While I applaud the readiness of the nonviolent protesters who were prepared to walk the streets and speak their truth, I believe that we can do more, in this opportune time, to prepare ourselves and our communities, so that we are more ready to address this pattern of violence in gracious and constructive ways.

At the beginning of 2015, I was in St. Louis giving a Holy Currencies workshop for the Midland Division Officers' Council of the Salvation Army. When the subject of Ferguson came up, I took the opportunity to do a holy currency analysis of the situation. I said, "Obviously, what has been happening in Ferguson is an indication that the community is not well. If we are to address this using the cycle of blessings, what do we need to do in order to foster wellness in Ferguson?"

The Salvation Army officers were no strangers to addressing community issues on ground level. They readily responded, "We need to have the currency of truth."

"We need to understand the issue from the perspective of the African American community with all of its history in that area." Another officer added, "And we need to understand this issue from the law enforcement's perspective as well. Right now, there are few opportunities for the truth to be spoken and heard since everything is so polarized."

"What do we need to do then in order to increase our currency of truth?" I continued the challenge.

"Rebuild trusting relationships among the police and the people in the community."

"What resources do you have to make this happen?" I asked.

The Midland Division has a beautiful camp and conference center in the St. Louis area. They have been planning a summer camp program that will invite police officers and community youth and young adults to spend a week together in a neutral setting to build trusting relationships, speak truth to each other, and cultivate wellness.

Finally I asked, "What currency do we need to ensure that when they are together in one place, they will speak respectfully and achieve mutual understanding in constructive ways?"

And they answered, "Gracious leadership." Having trained, gracious leaders to facilitate constructive dialogue will be essential for the success of this movement.

Truth events such as the one being planned by the Salvation Army of the Midland Division are what we need on a regular basis to prepare our selves, our neighborhoods, our towns, and our cities. These kinds of constructive dialogues among leaders in our communities, police departments, and justice system will help communities to arrive at concrete actions that can move people away from destructive, polarizing behaviors and toward constructive actions that foster wellness. If we want change, we must prepare ourselves to remain alert and act differently next time, or we are bound to repeat the same destructive pattern.

Beware, keep alert; for you do not know when the time will come. (Mark 13:33)

97

Stand Your Ground for Truth and Mercy

Mercy and truth are met together;
righteousness and peace have kissed each other.
Truth shall spring out of the earth;
and righteousness shall look down from heaven.
(Psalm 85:10–11, KJV)

Mercy, truth, righteousness, and peace—these words are rarely heard and experienced these days. Instead, vindictiveness, fabrication, malice, and hostility seem to be the order of the day, especially when something bad happens. The wonderful poetic lines from Psalm 85 tell us how our relationships with each other and with God can be restored, if we trust in God's grace to forgive us while keeping us accountable with the truth. Perhaps we will discern the right thing to do and peace among us will re-emerge.

However, instead of operating out of grace, our society has often given in to our fears—fear of those who are different, fear of being attacked, fear of being punished. This type of society is not sustainable, because no truth can be spoken in the midst of fear. Without truth, we don't know what is right, and there is no peace.

In the case of the so-called stand-your-ground law, we have put our fear into the law. This law was first enacted in Florida in 2005. Similar versions of Florida's law were adopted in at least 24 more states at the time of my writing this book. This law was used to justify the "not guilty" verdict of George Zimmerman, who shot an unarmed teenager, Trayvon Martin, on February 26, 2012. Read the first item of the original text of the law in Florida below:

776.013 Home protection; use of deadly force; presumption of fear of death or great bodily harm.—

(1) A person is presumed to have held a reasonable fear of imminent peril of death or great bodily harm to himself or herself or another when using defensive force that is intended or likely to cause death or great bodily harm to another if:

(a) The person against whom the defensive force was used was in the process of unlawfully and forcefully entering, or had unlawfully and forcibly entered, a dwelling, residence, or occupied vehicle, or if that person had removed or was attempting to remove another against that person's will from the dwelling, residence, or occupied vehicle; and

(b) The person who uses defensive force knew or had reason to believe that an unlawful and forcible entry or unlawful and forcible act was occurring or had occurred.

I am not saying that a society should have no laws that protect people. In fact, a law that truly protects people actually decreases our fear so that we can approach fellow members of society with trust, truth, and grace. But when a law is created out of fear and, in this case, actually propagates fears for others, such a fear-based society is not socially sustainable. So, don't stand your ground out of fear. Instead, stand your ground for mercy and truth. Stand your ground for righteousness and peace.

I invite you to read this law carefully and make up your own mind about where you stand and what you stand for.

Stand Your Ground

Gather members of your community to study and dialogue on the so-called Stand Your Ground law:

- Invite someone to read the text out loud.
- Invite participants to listen and capture a word ,phrase, or image that stands out for them.
- Using the "mutual invitation" process, invite participants to share their words, phrases, or images.
- Invite someone to read the text a second time.
- Invite participants to consider these questions:
  - What are the strengths of this law?
  - What are the weaknesses?
- Using the "mutual invitation" process, invite participants to share their reflections on these questions.
- Invite someone to read the text a third time.
- Invite participants to consider these questions as if they live in Florida or a state with the same law:
  - How might this law impact me personally?
  - How might this law impact my family?
  - How might this law impact my neighborhood community?
- Using the "mutual invitation" process, invite participants to share their reflections on these questions.
- Conclude the dialogue by asking participants to answer the following question:
  - As a result of the dialogue what am I called to do?

98

Ferguson Community Forum

Three weeks after the shooting of Michael Brown in Ferguson, Calvary Episcopal Church in Washington, D.C., under the leadership of the Rev. Peter Schell, organized a community forum to help people in the D.C. community to enter into gracious and constructive dialogue. Even though Washington, D.C., is more than 800 miles away from Ferguson, Peter took what was happening in Ferguson as an opportunity to bring local leaders together for a truth event in order to better prepare the community to face similar issues. The following is the report Peter wrote and posted on the internet.

In the wake of Michael Brown's shooting, Ms. Gayle Fisher-Stewart, a candidate for Holy Orders in the Diocese of Washington, the Rev. Rondesia Jarrett, Priest-in-Charge of Holy Communion Church, and myself met to discuss a possible response from within our Diocese. As we talked, it became clear that we had many more questions than answers. While there were many particular questions that arose in our conversation, the discussion crystalized around a single thought: "Could Ferguson happen here?" Could something like the Michael Brown killing occur here in D.C.? The question was fundamentally one of Police-Community relations. So, we decided that a public forum, involving members of the both the D.C. Police, and the community at large, would be the best place to begin our work.

We knew that a discussion of this nature would stir up a lot of feelings in everyone involved. We expected some heat, and anger. All three of us expressed feeling that anger ourselves. We knew this wasn't a bad thing. Anger can drive us to action. Indeed, we rushed our work in planning the forum, because we wanted to act before public outcry and outrage had cooled and faded. At the same time, we wanted to foster a productive dialogue. We wanted to be honest and frank with one another, without casting blame. To do this, we needed representatives from our Police Department. We had two specific blessings on this front. Ms. Fisher-Stewart is herself a retired member of the Washington Metropolitan Police Department, while the former Senior Warden of my congregation had served as the Assistant Chief of Police in D.C., and Chief of Police in two other major metropolitan areas. Both Ms. Fisher-Stewart and my former Senior Warden had been part of a national effort to move local law enforcement toward a model of community policing. Both had watched these efforts rolled back in recent years. Both were eager to participate in this dialogue.

We also approached the 1st and 7th Districts of the MPD—the districts where my congregation, Calvary Episcopal Church, and Holy Communion reside. We asked if they would send representatives to the forum. Both districts needed a little encouragement. We made our appeal: Even though the state of relations between the MPD and the community at large is generally positive, there are still areas of concern; and avoiding these difficult conversations is precisely what leads to suspicion between police and the community at large, in turn creating a dangerous environment for all involved. Both Districts agreed to send a representative.

We also approached several community organizations, to broaden the discussion. Ultimately, the Police Foundation and the National Organization of Black Law Enforcement Executives (NOBLE) agreed to send representatives. Our Bishop, the Right Rev. Mariann Budde, agreed to moderate. We publicized the event in the Diocese and our local neighborhoods, inviting folk to attend and to submit their questions for the panel in advance, via e-mail. Knowing that the discussion would be charged, and wanting to harness that fire without being consumed by it, we worked hard to organize the discussion in the most productive way possible. The Rev. Eric Law's book, *The Bush Was Blazing But Not Consumed*, provided great inspiration in outlining this process.

On the day of the forum, once the panelists and the community members were assembled, Rev. Jarrett opened us in prayer, asking for God's grace to do God's work, and asking everyone to share one word about how they felt as this discussion began. Then we laid out our purpose for the evening, in the following statements, which we provided in written form to everyone in attendance:

Tonight We Will:
- Discuss Whether or Not Ferguson Could Happen Here
- Share and Listen to All Perspectives
- Consider Best Practices for a Safe and Productive Relationship Between Police and the Community at Large
- Reflect on the Role of the Faith Community in This Effort
- Bless One Another

Tonight We Will Not:
- Seek to Place Blame
- Engage in Personal Attacks
- Monopolize Conversation
- Curse One Another

We also laid out our guidelines for discussion and communication:

Respectful Communication Guidelines

R - Accept RESPONSIBILITY for what you say and feel without blaming others.

E – Use EMPATHETIC listening.

S - Be SENSITIVE to differences in communication styles.

P - PONDER on what you hear and feel before you speak.

E - EXAMINE your own assumptions and perceptions.

C - Keep CONFIDENTIALITY.

T - TRUST ambiguity because we are not here to debate who is right or wrong.

(Reprinted from *The Bush Was Blazing But Not Consumed* by Eric Law)

We asked the participants and attendees to verbally affirm both our purposes for the evening and the communication guidelines, as a single body.

We posed the questions from members of the community to the panelists. These included both questions we had received in advance by e-mail, as well as those that participants were invited to submit on the spot, in writing. Ms. Fisher-Stewart, Rev. Jarrett, and I sorted and aggregated the questions before presenting them to the panelists. Our intent here was not to censor or redact in anyway, but simply to make good use of time. We expected, and were correct, that there would likely be many questions around the same themes. Aggregating the questions allowed us to address everyone's concerns in the time allotted.

After 45 minutes, we broke out into small groups, composed of both panelists and attendees together. Everyone was invited to complete the following statements, in their small groups:

Today I was struck by...

Today I learned...

After 15 minutes, each group was asked to suggest the next steps—for our police department, for our congregation, and for our community.

At the close of the forum, the small groups were invited to report back to the plenary session. While the responses were varied, two main themes emerged. The community at large needs more relational engagement from the police in the daily life of our neighborhoods, and the police need more active participation from the community when relations are problematic or strained.

Rev. Jarrett closed us in prayer, again asking all participants to share one word about how they felt, leaving the discussion that day. As we left, Ms. Fisher-Stewart shared one final thought: "The real work begins tomorrow."

99

Focus on the Baby

My niece gave birth to a beautiful baby in 2014. The whole family was excited and photos of the baby were filling our phones and electronic devices with the innocent, amazing image of a little human being.

Meanwhile, I was distracted by the civil war in Iraq, the Russian aggression in Ukraine, the flood of undocumented children crossing the border into the U.S., the growing tension between the law enforcement and the African American communities across the U.S., and the escalating conflict between Israel and Palestine (again). Who wins? Who loses? Who belongs? Who doesn't belong? Who has control over which land? Who has the right to claim what? Who lives? Who dies? These questions overwhelmed me, causing me to feel hopeless for a moment.

But then I stopped and said to myself, "Focus on the baby. Focus on the baby!" Things become simpler when we focus on the baby. A baby puts everything in perspective. A baby is disarming simply because she is completely trusting and dependent on the people around her. A baby doesn't care about whether he is documented or not. A baby does not ask whether she belongs or not. A baby just belongs. A baby looks at you and you know you have to share and give. A baby may seem completely helpless and yet a baby somehow sustains the people around him. Hold a baby in your arms and you will know what I mean.

There was no room at the inn, so Joseph and Mary occupied a stable or a cave somewhere in Bethlehem, probably illegally, and there she gave birth to the baby Jesus and put him in a manger. This is how the Christmas story is told in the gospel of Luke. God chose to come to us as a baby—not a powerful warrior, nor a king, nor a prophet, nor a high priest. Even though the baby may be small and helpless, he has power to capture everyone's attention, fascination, and imagination. A baby has a way of occupying completely her parents' hearts, minds, every thought, and even dreams. To hold a baby is to hold God in our arms, face-to-face, innocent and intimate. God, through a baby, calls for our attention, occupies our hearts and minds with hope, and generates new possibilities. Through a baby, we are reminded of the responsibilities that we have for what we are given—to move from scarcity (no room at the inn) to sustainability (community around a baby in a manger). Will you let God occupy your heart and mind like a baby occupies her parents' lives?

Baby

Invite members of your community to spend the coming week paying attention to babies especially when they can hold one for at least five minutes. Gather members of your community for a time of reflection with the following questions:

- What does a baby call us to do in order to create a sustainable future?
- At home?
- In our community?
- For the nation?
- For the earth?

100

The Occupy Song

Occupy my mind
With skill to tell what's true and right
So that I'm no longer blind
To the falsehood we must name and fight
The system shelters the rich
While the rest of us are down in the ditch
So occupy and stay...in my mind
In my mind

Occupy my heart
With passion for the common good
So that I will take my part
To rebuild a prosp'rous neighborhood
Where justice shines like the sun
and there's food and room for everyone
So occupy and stay...in my heart
In my heart

Occupy this place
With mercy, truth and liberty
So that we'll come face to face
With our friends and with our enemies
We'll listen, speak and we'll share
As we learn to do what's righteous and fair
So occupy and stay...in this place
In this place

The Occupy Song

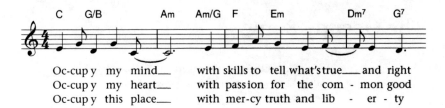

Oc-cup y my mind___ with skills to tell what's true___ and right
Oc-cup y my heart___ with pass ion for the com - mon good
Oc-cup y this place___ with mer-cy truth and lib - er - ty

so that I'm no long - er blind to the
so that I will take my part to re -
so that we'll come face to face with our

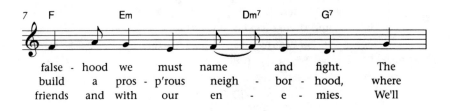

7

false - hood we must name and fight. The
build a pros - p'rous neigh - bor - hood, where
friends and with our en - e - mies. We'll

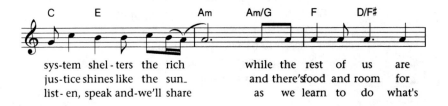

sys-tem shel - ters the rich while the rest of us are
jus-tice shines like the sun_ and there's food and room for
list- en, speak and we'll share as we learn to do what's

down in the ditch. So Oc-cup-y and stay in my
ev - er - y - one__ So Oc-cup-y and stay in my
right-eous and fair__ So Oc-cup-y and stay in this

mind,__ in my mind.
heart,__ in my heart.
place,__ in this place.

101

Leftover

The phone call came in December. "I need the address of the Kaleidoscope Institute so I can send you a check," the caller said to me. "What for?" I asked, because I could not remember doing anything for her organization within the last year.

"Oh," she replied, "My department has a leftover amount of money from this year's budget and my committee thought your organization should have it because of all the good things that you have done for us in the past."

December is also when some organizations that have contracted with the Kaleidoscope Institute for consultation and workshops in the following year insist on paying in full before the end of the current year. They sometimes say that the reason they can afford these future workshops is because they have leftover money in this year's budget.

When I was a child, the celebration of Chinese New Year's Eve always included a giant feast with the whole family. My mother would explain, "We have to make sure there is leftover for tomorrow, the New Year." Leftovers are a sign of abundance. The word for leftover or extra, 餘, sounds almost the same as the word for fish, 魚, in Cantonese. This is the reason why the image of the fish is found in many Chinese designs symbolizing blessings and abundance. And, of course, we always have fish soup as part of the New Year's Eve feast.

I started writing *The Sustainist,* my weekly blog, in 2011. When I began blogging, I had the fear that eventually I would run out of things to say. Yet, four years later, I am still writing. So much of my writing comes from my ministry through the Kaleidoscope Institute—training and coaching gracious leaders and consulting with local churches and ministries. In that sense, *The Sustainist* blog is the extra, the leftover that flows from the ministry of the Kaleidoscope Institute. If you have been a subscriber of *The Sustainist,* you know that the blog posts became the foundation of my book, *Holy Currencies: Six Blessings for Sustainable and Missional Ministries*. The abundance from the blog continues to flow, forming the body of this book.

Many of you have been subscribers of *The Sustainist* from the beginning. I thank you for your encouragement over the years. Some of you have also received resources from the Kaleidoscope Institute through our training institutes, locally facilitated classes, and consultations. Perhaps you have read *Holy Currencies*. Now that you have gotten this far with this book, what are the extras, the leftovers that flow from these resources for you? What are the holy currency exchanges?

As you approach the end of each year, I invite you to examine the past year and give thanks for the abundance that you have received. Then consider offering the leftover, the extra, to individuals and organizations as blessings. This way, you keep the blessings flowing for their families, friends, and communities for the coming year.

When they were satisfied, he told his disciples, "Gather up the fragments left over, so that nothing may be lost." (John 6:12)

Postlude: The Grace

The grace of our Lord, Jesus Christ
And the love of God
And the fellowship of the Holy Spirit
Be with us all
Be with us all
Evermore.
(2 Corinthians 13:14)

The Grace

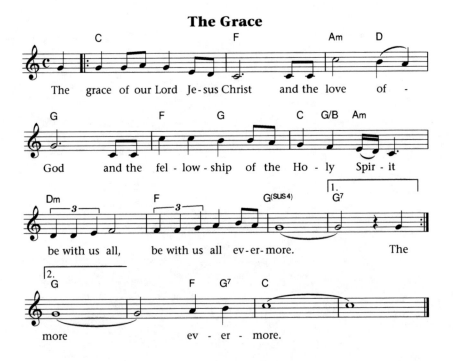

CPSIA information can be obtained
at www.ICGtesting.com
Printed in the USA
LVOW10s0552170418
573762LV00008B/244/P